THE LEGEND
OF
GODDESS BAGLAMUKHI

--- Weaving a Shield of Golden Light ---

Calling upon Maa Baglamukhi with the resonant power of
Her Ashtottara Shatanam Stotram

(Unveiling the Profound Secrets of the 108 Names of
the Divine Mother)

Authored by:
DEEPIKA ARORA

THE LEGEND OF GODDESS BAGLAMUKHI
Copyright © Deepika
All Rights Reserved

Disclaimer and Copyright

The author has made every possible effort to make this book error-free and informative. The interpretations and ideas presented herein are the result of the author's own original thinking and research, written with full respect toward all religions, communities, and personal beliefs. The purpose of sharing these interpretations is to provide a new perspective and support the reader's journey toward spiritual growth.

No part of this book may be reproduced or copied in any manner without the written permission of the author. The use of brief excerpts is permitted only in articles and reviews. Any resemblance to other works is entirely coincidental.

This book is based on the author's personal insights and is written for informational purposes only. It is not a substitute for health, medical, legal, or any kind of professional advice. It does not diagnose, treat, or prevent any condition.

By reading this book, you acknowledge that the author is not providing any spiritual, medical, health, or other professional services. The author shall not be liable for any personal loss, risk, or damage resulting from the use of the information provided.

The Expanded Edition: April, 2026

www.aroradeepika.com

"Whenever I feel restless or overwhelmed by the noise of the world, I close my eyes and simply find myself in the lap of the Universal Mother. In those few moments of stillness, a beautiful connection happens—I feel the embrace of the Divine Mother, the source of all existence, and, at the same time, I feel the presence of my own biological mother, who gave me this life and brought me into this world.

Resting in the shared consciousness of these two Mothers brings me a deep, unshakeable peace. It is not an escape from reality, but a way to recharge my spirit. It grounds me, clears my mind, and gives me the inner strength I need to tackle every challenge that comes my way. In their lap, I am reminded that no matter how difficult the situation is, I am always held, I am always safe, and I have the clarity to move forward."

This book is dedicated to you.

A NOTE TO THE SEEKERS

I spent twenty-five years of my life in North India, living not far from the sacred Baglamukhi Temple in Bankhandi, Himachal Pradesh. Growing up in the shadow of this powerful energy, I witnessed how deeply myths shape our perception of the Divine. To many, the name "Baglamukhi" carries a heavy, electrified charge—a name whispered with fearful reverence.

There is a pervasive belief that the Mother is a deity of kriyas—that she is a weapon to be wielded for Stambhan (pausing/freezing), Maranam (ending), Uchhatan (uprooting), or Mohanam (delusion). In this light, seekers often approach her looking for shortcuts, miraculous powers, or a desire to bring external circumstances under their control. But these ideas are based on deep-seated misconceptions. The true nature of these concepts is rarely understood, and the Mother's role is far more profound than we have been led to believe.

We must understand that the Mahavidyas—of which Maa Baglamukhi is a profound manifestation—are not entities of terror. They are the ten great facets of knowledge of this Universal Energy, each a unique expression of the same Divine Energy. By nurturing fear, we inadvertently build walls between ourselves and these sources of infinite wisdom. This fear is a screen, a self-imposed limitation that keeps the seeker from the light. I invite you to move beyond that fear, for the Mahavidyas are not here to threaten us; they are here to enlighten us.

The Mother is not a weapon of the ego, nor a force to be summoned for our own justifications. Often, we approach the Divine through the lens of our own insecurities—seeking a shield to deflect our enemies or a hand to perform miracles that bypass our own inner work. Baglamukhi does not exist to validate our fears; she exists to dissolve them, guiding us toward a truth that requires no defense.

She is the compassionate mother who understands the mechanism of our own self-destruction. She is the aspect of the Divine Feminine who empowers the voiceless. She is the energy that dismantles the irrational fears that hold us captive, granting us the unwavering courage to speak our truth, even when the world demands our silence. Her stillness is not passive; it is the foundation of our inner strength.

She does not harm even those we resent; rather, she offers the discipline of a mother, for they too are her children. She stills their inner turmoil, corrects their course, and grants them the wisdom they lack, or halts the chaos they create so that no further damage can be done. And should she choose to destroy, it is her sovereign call—a necessary dissolution born not of malice, but of divine timing. This is the true Baglamukhi aspect of universal energy—a Divine Intervention of Grace that protects us all by removing the obstacles within our own minds and the minds of others.

If you have picked up this book expecting a manual for miraculous powers, the practice of 'dark arts' to harm others, or ways to settle scores with those who have wronged you, I must be honest: this book will not meet your expectations. You will find no such weapons within these pages, as they have no place in the true essence of Maa Baglamukhi. This work is not written for the ego that seeks dominance; it is a devotional offering for the soul that seeks connection.

I felt a deep necessity to bring this work forth, to dismantle the walls of fear and superstition that have kept seekers from the Mother's true radiance. To help you move past this, I have explored 108 of her names. These are not magical spells for transactional gain, but a map of her nature. They are intended to help you understand who she is and what she actually does—to help you realize that she is not a goddess to be feared, but an energy to be invoked and experienced in our consciousness.

It is my sincere hope that this book liberates you from the shackles of superstition, guiding you out of the fog of fear and into the clear, luminous stillness of the Divine Mother. I pray that Devi Maa bless you, hold you in her grace, and illuminate your path toward the light.

With deepest reverence,

Deepika

ACKNOWLEDGEMENTS

This book owes its existence to the profound and ever-present influence of the Divine Source, the ultimate wellspring of inspiration and creativity. My deepest gratitude flows toward this guiding force that illuminated my path throughout this endeavor.

Furthermore, I extend my heartfelt appreciation to my family, mentors, and well-wishers. Their unwavering support and boundless love served as a constant source of strength and encouragement during the entire writing process. Their presence in my life has been an invaluable blessing.

PREFACE

Connecting with the energy of Maa Baglamukhi is not merely a path to attaining external powers; rather, it is a process of recognizing the immense power hidden within us, which keeps us steady in every adverse situation.

When I first started writing about this form of the Mother, my purpose was very simple—to dispel the misconceptions often woven around Her name. There is a common belief in society that Maa Baglamukhi is only a Goddess of 'Stambhan' (stilling) or 'display of power.' But through this Expanded Edition, I want to offer all readers a different perspective.

This book is not just a collection of mythological stories; rather, it is an attempt to weave a 'protective shield.' In this edition, I have added the experiences and research that I gathered during my writing journey. This book will teach you how, by letting go of the desire for external control, we can develop our inner peace and self-mastery.

In this journey, you will understand that the true meaning of the Mother's grace is not the destruction of enemies, but the calming of those internal enemies—such as fear, doubt, and confusion—that hinder our progress.

I have strived to keep this book extremely simple and close to the heart, so that any seeker or devotee who wishes to walk this path can establish a personal and deep connection with the Mother.

This book is not just mine; it belongs to all those who are in search of truth and who wish to face life's challenges with an empowered and divine perspective. I trust that this 'Expanded Edition' will act as a guide in your spiritual journey.

May your spiritual journey be auspicious.

— Deepika

CONTENTS

Embark on a journey to understand the powerful Goddess Baglamukhi. Discover her core mysteries and the significance of her 108 names. Explore her place within broader spirituality, her enduring legacy, and her intricate link to the body's chakras.

This section introduces the fundamental aspects and enigmatic nature of Goddess Baglamukhi, laying the groundwork for deeper understanding.

This part offers an in-depth examination of the 108 names of Goddess Baglamukhi, revealing their significance and multifaceted attributes.

This section focuses on specific practices and rituals associated with Goddess Baglamukhi, offering insights into how devotees connect with her.

This part illuminates the relationship between Goddess Baglamukhi and the body's energy centers (chakras), revealing potential connections and influences.

PITAMBARA - PITAMBARA

"Seeking refuge in the golden embrace of Baglamukhi, the fierce protector who paralyzes all that seeks to harm and the one who empowers us to stand fearless...."

ABOUT THE BOOK

This book is a humble attempt to explore the multifaceted nature of Goddess Baglamukhi, a prominent but somewhat mysterious figure in the Hindu pantheon. It delves into her mythology, symbolism, worship, and enduring relevance, aiming to provide a comprehensive understanding of her significance. This work is not intended to be an exhaustive academic treatise but rather a devotional offering, combining scholarly research with personal insights and experiences. It seeks to illuminate the unique power and grace of Baglamukhi. The book also addresses some of the misconceptions surrounding her, particularly those related to her association with Tantra, by presenting a balanced and authentic perspective. At its heart, this book delves into the profound meanings embedded within the Ashtottara Shatanam Stotram of Maa Baglamukhi, directly from the revered Rudrayamala Tantra, which can be chanted by anyone with devotion and sincerity; no prior initiation is required.

Goddess Baglamukhi holds a unique and powerful position in Hinduism, particularly within the Tantric tradition. She is revered as one of the ten Mahavidyas, the wisdom goddesses, and is primarily associated with the power of stambhana, which translates to "paralyzing" or "immobilizing." This power is often invoked to silence enemies, quell doubts, and overcome obstacles, both internal and external. Her significance extends beyond mere protection; she is also seen as a force for truth, justice, and the restoration of balance. She is considered a powerful deity for those seeking to overcome adversity, legal troubles, and personal conflicts. Baglamukhi's energy is believed to help devotees gain control over their speech, thoughts, and actions, leading to clarity and self-mastery.

According to a legend, Maa Baglamukhi is considered to be a form of Tripura Sundari. During the Satya Yuga, a massive storm threatened the universe, compelling Lord Vishnu to seek the aid of Tripura Sundari. Vishnu performed intense penance on the banks of the Haridra Sarovar (a lake filled with turmeric). Pleased by his deep devotion, Tripura Sundari manifested as Baglamukhi and emerged from the lake. Subsequently, Goddess Baglamukhi calmed the fierce storm, restoring peace and order throughout the entire universe.

My journey with Goddess Baglamukhi began during a period of intense personal struggle. I was confronted with overwhelming negativity, both from external sources and internal turmoil. In search of solace and a way to overcome these challenges, I visited the Baglamukhi Temple in Himachal Pradesh. The visit to this sacred place, coupled with the practice of chanting her sacred names, brought about a profound sense of peace and resilience. This experience ignited a deep curiosity to learn more about this powerful deity. During this time, I also had the opportunity to study the profound teachings of the Lalita Sahasranama and Sri Vidya and to incorporate those practices into my spiritual journey. This broader understanding of the divine feminine, and its various manifestations, has further enriched my connection with Goddess Baglamukhi.

This book is the result of that curiosity, coupled with a desire to share the transformative power of Baglamukhi with others who may be facing similar challenges. It is a humble offering born out of a personal journey of seeking and finding refuge in the divine embrace of Goddess Baglamukhi. It is my hope that by sharing my own experiences and insights, I can help others connect with Baglamukhi's energy and find the same strength and guidance that I did.

This book is intended for a diverse audience, including devotees of Goddess Baglamukhi seeking a deeper understanding of her mythology and practices; spiritual seekers interested in exploring the Tantric traditions and the Mahavidyas; individuals facing challenges and seeking divine intervention and guidance;

and scholars interested in learning about lesser-known aspects of Hindu deities.

Readers can expect to gain a comprehensive understanding of Goddess Baglamukhi, including her mythological origins and symbolism; exploring the divine narratives associated with her emergence and the deeper symbolic meanings behind her iconography and attributes; detailed descriptions of her various forms, the objects she holds, and their significance in understanding her powers and functions; a practical guide to invoking her energy through sacred names without initiation, exploring how Baglamukhi's energy relates to the body's energy centers and how to work with this connection for personal transformation; and guidance on how to integrate Baglamukhi's teachings and practices into everyday life to overcome challenges, enhance self-control, and achieve desired outcomes.

It is my hope that this book will serve as a source of knowledge, inspiration, and solace, guiding readers on their own journey of self-discovery and empowerment through the divine grace of Goddess Baglamukhi.

PART 1

Delving into the Mysteries of Goddess Baglamukhi

The Divine Feminine and the Mahavidyas

The Eternal Pulse of Shakti: The Heart of Existence

In the vast and intricate landscape of Hinduism, we do not merely see the world as matter; we experience it as Shakti. Observing the rhythms of life, I see Shakti as the dynamic, breathing energy that is inherent in every corner of the universe. She is the heartbeat in the silence. It is a common misconception to view the divine feminine as separate from the masculine; in truth, she is the very power of manifestation that allows masculine consciousness to act.

Without Shakti, the divine consciousness remains a dormant potential, a silent observer. She is the architect who builds, the mother who nurtures, and the force of nature that eventually reclaims. Various goddesses are worshipped as the embodiment of this power, but they are all rivers flowing from the same infinite ocean of Shakti. She is the power behind the rising sun, the shifting tides, and the very spark of life within us.

The Mahavidyas: An Odyssey of Great Wisdom

The **Mahavidyas** represent a profound journey into the ten Great Wisdoms of the universe. The word "Mahavidya" is derived from Maha (Great) and Vidya (Wisdom or Knowledge). These ten goddesses are not just figures of myth; they are Tantric keys that unlock the deepest chambers of the human soul. They are known for their fierce, unconventional, and sometimes startling forms—forms that are intended to shatter our narrow perceptions of 'good' and 'evil'.

Each goddess is a unique manifestation of Shakti, guiding the devotee toward spiritual liberation and worldly mastery. They are the ten paths to the same mountain peak:

Kali: The Truth of Time, who reminds us that all ego must eventually perish.

Tara: The Compassionate Savior, who guides us through the turbulent waters of life.

Tripura Sundari (Shodashi): The radiant perfection of the three worlds, representing the beauty of the soul.

Bhuvaneshvari: The Cosmic Queen whose body is the very space we inhabit.

Tripura Bhairavi: The fierce flame of transformation that burns away impurity.

Chhinnamasta: The self-surrendering goddess who teaches us to transcend the mind.

Dhumavati: The Smoky Widow, representing the wisdom found in solitude and disappointment.

Baglamukhi: The Stunner, the one who brings the universe to a standstill.

Matangi: The goddess of inner speech and the raw power of the arts.

Kamalatmika: The Lotus Goddess, the manifestation of grace and worldly abundance.

These goddesses represent the full, unedited spectrum of the Divine Feminine—from the gentle, honey-like nurturing of a mother to the terrifying, bone-chilling roar of a warrior. They offer us a map to understand that reality is multifaceted and that the divine resides even in the shadows.

Baglamukhi's Specialized Throne

Within this sacred circle, Baglamukhi occupies the eighth position, a station of immense strategic power. She is the mistress of Stambhana—a Sanskrit term signifying the act of paralyzing, stopping, or restraining. While other manifestations of the Divine might choose to destroy or transform, Baglamukhi masters the art of the 'Divine Pause.' She is the one who freezes an enemy mid-strike, silences a slanderer mid-sentence, and brings an obstacle to a complete standstill. She is distinct among the Mahavidyas for this specific ability to immobilize, proving that sometimes the ultimate victory is won not in the clash of battle, but in the absolute cessation of all movement.

Who is Baglamukhi?

Etymology of Baglamukhi: Exploring the meaning of "Bagla" and "Mukhi"

The very name Baglamukhi embodies an ancient authority. It is widely believed by scholars and practitioners that the name evolved from the Sanskrit word Valga, which means "bridle" or "rein"—the very tools used to control and direct a powerful horse. Over centuries of devotion, Valgamukhi transitioned into the name we know today. This tells us everything about her essence: she is the goddess who holds the reins of the universe. She is the one who can pull back on the momentum of fate and bring even the most chaotic forces under control.

There is also a profound link to the Crane (Bagala). In nature, the crane is a master of patience and focus. It stands on one leg in the water, perfectly motionless, appearing almost as part of the landscape. This aligns perfectly with the Goddess's role—she provides the focus and the auspiciousness required to overcome challenges not through frantic effort, but through the power of centered stillness.

The Iconography of the Golden Queen

When we envision Baglamukhi, we see a world drenched in yellow. She is the Pitambara Devi, the one who is clad in the color of the sun and turmeric. She has a radiant, golden complexion that seems to emit its own light. She is often depicted sitting upon a golden throne in the midst of a sea of yellow lotuses.

Her most impactful and fierce form is manifested in her control over the adversary. She is shown holding a demon by the tongue with her left hand, while her right hand is raised, holding a massive mace (Gada). This is a moment frozen in time—the demon is silenced, paralyzed, and completely at her mercy.

The Symbolism of Her Sacred Attributes

The Color Yellow: This is not merely a cosmetic choice. Yellow is the color of the sun, of light, and of the intellect. It represents the "Tejas" or the spiritual fire that purifies the soul. It is associated with the earth element, providing a grounded, stable energy that is required for effective "Stambhana."

The Pulled Tongue: This is perhaps the most significant symbol in her iconography. The tongue is the organ of speech—our primary interface with the world—but it is also the frequent source of negative karma born from lies and insults. By pulling the tongue, the Goddess does not merely silence; she stills the root of conflict. She reminds us that the mastery of one's speech is the mastery of one's destiny.

The Mace (Gada): The club represents the crushing weight of divine justice. It is the tool she uses to break the stubbornness of the ego and to shatter the obstacles that block the devotee's path.

Her Posture: Her entire presence conveys a sense of absolute, unshakeable control. It illustrates a vital spiritual truth: that inner peace and self-mastery are the ultimate weapons. When you are centered, you do not need to shout to be heard; your very presence can silence the world.

Manifestations and Forms

Pitambara Devi

She is widely known as **Pitambara Devi** (The Goddess Clad in Yellow). This name emphasizes her role as a beacon of light and energy, specifically the "yellow" energy used in Tantric rituals to stabilize and protect.

Vak Stambhanakari

She is also revered as **Vak Stambhanakari**—the one who paralyzes speech. In ancient traditions, "Vak" (speech) is the most powerful tool of a human; by controlling speech, Baglamukhi controls the very essence of human action and intention.

The Internal Battlefield: Reversing the Current of Negativity

We often look at the stories of Baglamukhi as a way to defeat external enemies, but walking this path, I invite you to look deeper. The true "demons" (asurs) are not people outside of us; they are the shadows that live within our own minds. When we invoke the Goddess, we are asking her to freeze the chaos inside so that the external world naturally settles into peace.

The Principle (Tattva) of Universal Energy

It is essential to understand that the Mahavidyas are not just separate entities; they are roles played by the one Universal Energy. When we speak of Baglamukhi, we are speaking of a Tattva—a fundamental Essence or Principle of the universe. The practice of Mahavidya Sadhana is a method of invocation; it is the way we awaken that specific "stillness," "transformation" or "destruction" within our own DNA. By attuning to her frequency, we are not merely reaching out to a distant deity, but unlocking a dormant potential that has always resided within the architecture of our consciousness. It is the profound realization that the Divine is not an external observer, but the very intelligence living and breathing through the fabric of our own existence.

The Origin: A Manifestation of Tripurasundari

A profound aspect of this lineage is that Maa Baglamukhi manifests from the essence of Tripurasundari, the Goddess of the **"Three Worlds."** These worlds are not distant, external realms; they are the three states of our own consciousness:

The Waking State (Jagrat): Our conscious mind, through which we interact with the physical world.

The Dream State (Swapna): Our subconscious mind, where our hidden desires and anxieties play out.

The Deep Sleep State (Sushupti): Our unconscious mind, the deep, silent reservoir of our being.

Because she arises from this fundamental source, Baglamukhi's energy permeates all three layers of our existence. When we focus on her, we send a profound signal to our psyche that it is time to awaken the power of restraint. We invite her Tattva—the very essence of her truth—into the depths of our consciousness, transforming how we perceive and respond to our own reality.

The Internal "Asurs" (Demons) She Immobilizes

The Goddess of Stambhana is revered for her unique power to paralyze the forces that obstruct our spiritual growth. These internal adversaries are all born from the root demon: **Ignorance**.

Ignorance: This is the fundamental delusion that causes us to mistake the temporary for the eternal. Since Baglamukhi is a "Great Wisdom," her ultimate act is to paralyze this ignorance, stopping the cycle of false perception.

Ego and Pride: This is the psychological barrier that prevents us from learning and growing. By restraining the ego, the Goddess immobilizes our need for external validation, fostering a state of true humility (Vinamrata).

Attachment and Clinging: This demon manifests as the emotional "glue" that binds us to outcomes and possessions. Baglamukhi's power freezes this clinging, allowing us to act in the world with peace and detachment.

Greed and Insatiable Desire: This is the hunger that drives unethical behavior. By paralyzing Greed, she stabilizes our desires, ensuring our actions are driven by righteousness (Dharma).

Fear and Doubt: These are the killers of action. They paralyze our will. Baglamukhi's power stops this fear from rising, freezing our hesitation and freeing our energy to move forward.

Anger and Hatred: Anger is a fire that burns up our wisdom. By freezing this demon, she ensures the mind remains cool and steady, even in the face of provocation.

Jealousy and Comparison: This demon drains our energy by focusing it on others. The Goddess neutralizes this toxic comparison, allowing us to focus on our own self-improvement.

Laziness and Procrastination: This is the inertia of the mind. The Goddess uses her power to immobilize this lethargy, pushing us toward active, righteous effort.

When we awaken Baglamukhi within, she successfully "Stambha" (immobilizes) all these binding forces. This is the internal mastery that must always come before external victory.

The Secret of Aura Cleaning (Energy Cleansing)

The icons of the **Mace** and the **Pulled Tongue** are not just ancient art; they are symbols of profound **Mental Peace**. When our internal negative forces are stopped, we begin the process of cleansing our aura—our Urja Kshetra (Energy Field). What does it mean to clean an aura through Baglamukhi?— It means that our inner peace and confidence become so strong that they begin to cleanse the space around you.

The Power of Stillness: When our aura is clean and strong, the opposition naturally becomes silent.

The Shield of Truth: The opposition is silenced because their lies or wrong intentions clash with our clean energy and are "frozen" right there. The power to silence an enemy does not come from attacking them; it is born from our own internal stillness and the courage to speak our truth.

One Power, Many Roles—the question then becomes: how do we begin the method to attain this Aura Cleaning and Mental Peace? The answer lies in the sacred verses of the Baglamukhi Ashtottara Shatanam Stotram.

Legends and Myths: The Narrative of Her Might

Manifestation from Haridra Sarovar

The stories of her origin are as golden as her complexion. During the Satya Yuga, a cosmic storm of unimaginable power arose, threatening to tear the fabric of creation apart. Lord Vishnu, the Preserver of the Universe, watched in distress as the world he guarded began to crumble. He realized that no ordinary force could stop this destruction.

In his desperation, Vishnu performed intense and arduous tapas (austerities) to appease the Supreme Goddess, **Tripura Sundari**. He poured his heart and devotion into his penance for a long time. Pleased by his unwavering focus, the Mother manifested from the **Haridra Sarovar**—a lake in Saurashtra, Gujarat, filled with golden turmeric. As Baglamukhi stepped out of the yellow waters, the storm began to lose its strength. Her very presence calmed the turbulent energies of the cosmos. This story is a beautiful reminder of her power to quell any disturbance and restore balance when life feels chaotic. Just as she emerged from those golden waters to still the cosmic tempest, she stands ready to emerge within the sanctuary of our own hearts during our most turbulent hours. Her arrival acts as the 'pause button' of the soul, transforming the clamor of our worldly battles into the golden silence of her divine grace.

The Silence of the Demon Madan

Another legend tells of a demon named Madan, who held a unique boon called Vak-siddhi. This meant that whatever he spoke would immediately come true. Imagine the terror of such power in the hands of one filled with arrogance! He used his words to spread fear and disrupt the natural order.

The gods and humanity were helpless; for every time they tried to stop him, he simply spoke their defeat into existence. They prayed to Baglamukhi for intervention. When she appeared, she did not engage in a long battle of weapons; she simply reached out and seized his tongue. By immobilizing his organ of speech, she neutralized his power instantly. In his final moments, Madan realized her greatness and requested that he be remembered alongside her. Out of her infinite compassion, she granted him this, which is why he is seen at her feet in her worship. This story teaches us that she is the ultimate protector against those who misuse the power of words.

The Retrieval of the Vedas: Brahma's Plea

There is a lesser-known story of a demon who managed to steal the holy Vedas from Lord Brahma, the creator. The Vedas represent the fundamental knowledge of the universe; without them, the world is plunged into a state of spiritual ignorance.

Brahma, in deep distress, sought the help of the Divine Mother. She manifested as Baglamukhi and took the form of a crane. With the precision and focus that only she possesses, she pursued the demon, engaged him in a fierce battle, and ultimately annihilated him. She retrieved the stolen knowledge and returned it to Brahma, ensuring that the light of wisdom would continue to shine. This highlights her role as the guardian of sacred knowledge. This story signifies Baglamukhi's role in protecting sacred knowledge and restoring balance when it is disrupted.

Lord Rama's Devotion and the Brahmastra

In the epic Ramayana, we find another testament to her power. During the final, grueling battle against the demon king Ravana, Lord Rama—despite being an avatar of Vishnu—felt the immense weight of Ravana's dark power. Ravana was a formidable adversary, and the war was a battle for the very soul of righteousness.

Guided by the wisdom of Hanuman, Lord Rama worshipped Goddess Baglamukhi. He recognized that to defeat such a powerful enemy, he needed the divine power of "Stambhana." Pleased by his sincere devotion and the righteousness of his cause, Baglamukhi granted him the Brahmastra. This was not just a weapon; it was a celestial instrument of unparalleled power, capable of freezing and destroying negative energies. With this divine gift, Rama was able to overcome Ravana and ensure that Dharma prevailed. This story underscores that her blessings are available to all who fight for truth and righteousness.

Other relevant stories and references from scriptures

While the stories mentioned above are the most prominent, other stories and references to Baglamukhi can be found in various Tantric texts and Puranas. These texts often contain more detailed accounts of her powers, her various forms, and the rituals associated with her worship. However, those stories are less widely known or circulated compared to the popular legends.

PART 2

The Baglamukhi Ashtottara Shatanam Stotram: A Comprehensive Exploration

In the vast and intricate tapestry of Hindu Tantra, where divine energies manifest in myriad forms to guide and protect humanity, Goddess Baglamukhi stands as a resplendent and formidable force. As one of the ten wisdom goddesses, the Das Mahavidyas, she embodies the power to paralyze negativity, silence adversaries, and reverse harmful intentions. Her very presence radiates a potent energy capable of stilling the storms of life and granting victory over challenges. While her multifaceted nature can be approached through various powerful mantras and intricate rituals, the Baglamukhi Ashtottara Shatanam Stotram offers a direct and accessible pathway to connect with her divine essence.

This sacred compilation, a garland of 108 auspicious names, each resonating with a specific facet of the Goddess's power and glory, serves as a profound tool for devotion, contemplation, and the invocation of her blessings. More than just a recitation of names, the Ashtottara Shatanam Stotram is a vibrant tapestry woven with the threads of Baglamukhi's myriad attributes, her fierce compassion and her unwavering commitment to upholding righteousness. Each name acts as a key, unlocking a particular aspect of her being – her role as the dispeller of darkness, the bestower of courage, the granter of control, and the ultimate protector against all that seeks to harm or hinder our spiritual and worldly progress.

Within these 108 Divine Names lies a profound understanding of Baglamukhi's cosmic function and her intimate connection with the individual devotee. Chanting these names with devotion and sincerity creates a powerful resonance, drawing the seeker into her protective embrace and imbuing them with her formidable energy.

Unlike some advanced practices that require specific initiations, the Baglamukhi Ashtottara Shatanam Stotram holds a unique accessibility, allowing anyone, regardless of their spiritual background or prior training, to directly invoke the Goddess's grace simply through heartfelt recitation. It is a testament to her boundless compassion that even the sincere utterance of her sacred names can pave the way for overcoming obstacles, achieving success, and experiencing profound positive transformation in the journey of life. This text serves as an invitation to explore this potent and readily available pathway to connect with the invincible power and benevolent grace of Maa Baglamukhi.

Within the pages of this present work, let's delve deeply into the heart of this sacred tradition by offering a meticulous and detailed interpretation of the 19 seminal verses that encapsulate the Baglamukhi Ashtottara Shatanam Stotram. These verses form the bedrock of this devotional practice, not only reverently enumerating the 108 sacred names of the Divine Mother Baglamukhi but also crucially incorporating the 'Phala Shruti' – the traditional and eloquent articulation of the manifold blessings, spiritual merits, and auspicious outcomes bestowed upon the sincere devotee through its recitation. My endeavor is to illuminate the profound significance and potent energy inherent in each of these verses, thereby enriching the devotee's understanding and deepening their connection to the Goddess.

BAGLAMUKHI ASHTOTTARA SHATANAM STOTRAM

Om Sarv Gurubhyo Namah
Om Sri Ganeshaya Namah
Om Kuldevtabhayo Namah
Om Kuldeviye Namah
Om Matra-Pitra Devbhayo Namah
Om Bhairvaye Namah

Brahmāstrarupiṇī Devī Mātā Śrībagalāmukhī |
Cicchiktirjñāna-Rupā Ca Brahmānanda-Pradāyinī || 1 ||

Mahāvidyā Mahālakṣmī Śrīmattripurasundarī |
Bhuvaneśī Jaganmātā Pārvatī Sarvamangalā || 2 ||

Lalitā Bhairavī Śāntā Annapūrṇā Kuleśvarī |
Vārāhī Chinnamastā Ca Tārā Kālī Sarasvatī || 3 ||

Jagatpūjyā Mahāmāyā Kāmeśī Bhagamālinī |
Dakṣaputrī Śivānkasthā Śivarupā Śivapriyā || 4 ||

Sarva-Sampatkarī Devī Sarvaloka Vaśankarī |
Vedavidyā Mahāpūjyā Bhaktādveṣī Bhayankarī || 5 ||

Stambha-Rupā Stambhinī Ca Duṣṭastambhanakāriṇī |
Bhaktapriyā Mahābhogā Śrīvidyā Lalitāmbikā || 6 ||

Maināputrī Śivānandā Mātangī Bhuvaneśvarī |
Nārasiṃhī Narendrā Ca Nṛpārādhyā Narottamā || 7 ||

Nāginī Nāgaputrī Ca Nagarājasutā Umā |
Pītāmbā Pītapuṣpā Ca Pītavastrapriyā Śubhā || 8 ||

Pītagandhapriyā Rāmā Pītaratnārcitā Śivā |
Arddhacandradharī Devī Gadāmudgaradhāriṇī || 9 ||

Sāvitrī Tripadā Śuddhā Sadyorāga Vivardhinī |
Viṣṇurupā Jaganmohā Brahmarupā Haripriyā || 10 ||

Rudrarupā Rudraśaktiścinmayī Bhaktavatsalā |
Lokamātā Śivā Sandhyā Śivapūjanatatparā || 11 ||

Dhanādhyakṣā Dhaneśī Ca Dharmadā Dhanadā Dhanā |
Caṇḍadarpaharī Devī Śumbhāsuranibarhiṇī || 12 ||

Rājarājeśvarī Devī Mahiṣāsuramardinī |
Madhūkaiṭabhahantrī Devī Raktabījavināśinī || 13 ||

Dhūmrākṣadaityahantrī Ca Bhaṇḍāsura Vināśinī |
Reṇuputrī Mahāmāyā Bhrāmarī Bhramarāmbikā || 14 ||

Jvālāmukhī Bhadrakālī Bagalā Śatrunāśinī |
Indrāṇī Indrapūjyā Ca Guhamātā Guṇeśvarī || 15 ||

Vajrapāśadharā Devī Jhvāmudgaradhāriṇī |
Bhaktānandakarī Devī Bagalā Parameśvarī || 16 ||

Aṣṭottaraśataṃ Nāmnāṃ Bagalāyāstu Yaḥ Paṭhet |
Ripubādhāvinirmuktaḥ Lakṣmīsthairyamavāpnuyāt
|| 17 ||

Bhūtapretapiśācāśca Grahapīḍaānivāraṇam |
Rājāno Vaśamāyānti Sarvaiśvaryaṃ Ca Vindati || 18 ||

Nānāvidyāṃ Ca Labhate Rājyaṃ Prāpnoti Niścitam |
Bhuktimuktimavāpnoti Sākṣāt Śivasamo Bhavet || 19 ||

|| Iti Śrī Rudrayāmale Sarva-Siddhi-Prada Bagalā'Ṣṭottara-Śatanāma-
Stotram ||

This is the all-pervading Bagla Ashtottara Shatanaama Stotram in Sri
Rudra Yamala.

VERSE 1

ब्रह्मास्त्ररुपिणी देवी माता श्रीबगलामुखी ।
चिच्छक्तिर्ज्ञान-रुपा च ब्रह्मानन्द-प्रदायिनी ॥ १ ॥

Brahmāstrarupiṇī Devī Mātā Śrībagalāmukhī ।
Cicchiktirjñāna-Rupā Ca Brahmānanda-Pradāyinī ॥ 1 ॥

हे ब्रह्मास्त्र के समान सामर्थ्यवान, ज्ञान और चेतना शक्ति की साकार रूप, देवी माता श्री बगलामुखी! आपकी कृपा से भक्त आध्यात्मिक ज्ञान प्राप्त करते हैं। आप ब्रह्मानंद की प्रदात्री हैं, जिसके आशीर्वाद से आत्मिक शांति और आनंद की अनुभूति होती है।

You are as powerful as the Brahmastra, the Mother Goddess Shri Baglamukhi who is the embodiment of Chichchakti (consciousness power) and knowledge by whose blessings the devotees attain spiritual knowledge. You bestows Brahmananda (supernatural bliss) whose blessings lead to a feeling of spiritual peace and joy..

The Cosmic Crisis: A Twilight of the Soul

To grasp the necessity of **Mātā Śrī Bagalāmukhī's** descent, we must look beyond the physical world and into the subtle, shivering realms of the spirit. There are moments in the history of existence marked by profound cosmic disharmony—times not defined by the clash of falling swords, but by a chilling, pervasive silence of the soul. It is a darkness of the intellect, a spiritual twilight where the light of consciousness begins to flicker and fade.

In this heavy atmosphere, falsehoods do not merely exist; they thrive. They bloom like toxic, night-flowering vines that choke the life out of truth. The path to understanding, once clear and bright, becomes a web of mirrors and deceptive echoes. Even the most dedicated seekers find their spirits dampened, yearning for the sunlight of enlightenment but finding only a fog of collective delusion. These "asurs" of ego and deception whisper that the darkness is the only reality, creating a crisis of the spirit that requires more than a miracle—it requires an absolute, crushing force of Truth.

The Radiant Manifestation: The Brahmastra in Golden Flesh

Into this suffocating gloom, a radiant, golden energy erupts from the very core of the Divine Heart. This is the manifestation of the Mother. She does not appear as a passive observer, but as **Brahmāstrarupiṇī**—the Goddess whose very essence, whose every atom, is the **Brahmastra**.

In the ancient sciences of the soul, the Brahmastra is the weapon of last resort, a force so potent that it cannot be turned back, cannot be countered, and cannot fail. Yet, in the hands of the Mother, this weapon is not a tool of annihilation, it is an instrument of surgical precision. She is the divine weapon that strikes not at the flesh, but at the root of the lie. Her golden form is the antidote to the poisonous flowers of falsehood. When she stands before us, her radiance acts as an unstoppable wave of clarity, stripping away the veils of Maya until only the naked truth remains. Just as the

Brahmastra settles a war in a single heartbeat, Baglamukhi settles the war within the mind with a single golden glance.

Cicchakti: The Pulse of Pure Consciousness

The verse reveals that the Mother is **Cicchiktirjñāna-Rupā**. She is the embodiment of Chichchakti—the dynamic, vibrating power of Pure Consciousness. She is not merely a teacher of knowledge; she is the very form of knowledge itself. Every movement of her hand, every breath she takes, is a manifestation of the highest wisdom.

She is the wellspring from which all true understanding flows. While the world offers us "information," Baglamukhi offers us "illumination." She is the frequency that allows the human mind to tune into the divine broadcast. Her golden light is a beacon that does not just shine on us; it shines through us, piercing the shadows of our internal ignorance. She is the power that allows us to look at the most complex deception and say, with absolute certainty, "This is not real." She provides the Stambhana (paralysis) of the ego, stopping the frantic, anxious movement of the lower mind so that the higher mind can finally ascend to its rightful throne.

The Gift of Brahmananda: The Transcendent Joy

The promise of this sacred verse is that she is the **Brahmānanda-Pradāyinī**—the Giver of the Bliss of the Infinite. This Brahmananda is fundamentally different from the "pleasures" we chase in our daily lives. Worldly happiness is like a candle flame—easily flickered and eventually extinguished by the winds of change.

The bliss that the Mother bestows is like the sun—constant, self-sustaining, and vast. This is the joy of the soul realizing its own divinity. It is the radiance that comes when the heavy chains of "I" and "Mine" are finally broken by the blow of her golden mace. In her infinite compassion, she realizes that we cannot find this joy while we are being haunted by the ghosts of past karma or the demons of future anxiety. Therefore, she uses her power to "still" the distractions, creating a sacred, silent space within the heart where the individual consciousness can finally merge with the Universal, experiencing a peace that passes all understanding.

The Seeker's Journey: From Shadows to Certainty

Picture a weary traveler who has spent lifetimes lost in a dense forest of mental confusion. The trees are twisted into the shapes of his own fears; the ground is soft with the rot of old regrets. Deceptive lights flicker in the distance, leading him further away from the home she can barely remember.

Suddenly, the sky opens, and the Mother descends as a pillar of brilliant, golden fire. She does not just show the traveler a map; she becomes the light. Under her gaze, the deceptive shadows do not just flee—they cease to exist. She empowers the seeker with the **Jñāna** (knowledge) to see the forest for what it is: a mere play of light and shadow. By her grace, the traveler is no longer a victim of the forest. He attains an inner stillness so profound that even if the forest remains, its power to confuse her is gone forever. This is the Stambhana of the world's influence over the soul.

The Final Essence: The Key to the Divine

In conclusion, we must revere **Maa Baglamukhi** not just as a figure of ancient wisdom, but as the living embodiment of the **Brahmastra** in its highest spiritual form. She is the bridge between our confusion and our clarity. She is the very power of consciousness and the sword of knowledge that severs the knots of our hearts.

Her blessings are the essential key to unlocking the mysteries of our own existence. When we call upon the **Brahmāstrarupiṇī**, we are calling upon the universe's most powerful force to intervene in our spiritual journey—to dispel our darkness, to paralyze our internal enemies, and to finally lead us into the radiant, golden embrace of **Brahmananda**. She is the mother who silences the noise of the world so that we may finally hear the song of our own eternal soul.

VERSE 2

महाविद्या महालक्ष्मी श्रीमत्त्रिपुरसुन्दरी ।
भुवनेशी जगन्माता पार्वती सर्वमंगला ॥ २ ॥

Mahāvidyā Mahālakṣmī Śrīmattripurasundarī ।
Bhuvaneśī Jaganmātā Pārvatī Sarvamangalā ॥ 2 ॥

आप ही महाविद्या (दिव्य ज्ञान और शक्ति के उच्चतम स्वरूप), महालक्ष्मी (धन, समृद्धि, और कल्याण की देवी) और श्रीमत त्रिपुरसुंदरी (सौंदर्य, ज्ञान, और पूर्णता की प्रतीक) हैं, भुवनेशी, जगत की माता हैं, पार्वती - सभी के लिए शुभ और मंगलकारी हैं

You are Mahavidya (the highest form of divine knowledge and power), Mahalakshmi (the goddess of wealth, prosperity, and well-being) and Shrimat Tripursundari (the epitome of beauty, knowledge, and perfection), Bhuvaneshi, the mother of the world, Parvati — the embodiment of all. You are auspicious for all..

The Universal Tapestry: One Light, Many Hues

Imagine the entire cosmos not as a cold vacuum of space, but as a vast and intricate tapestry, woven with luminous threads of knowledge, power, beauty, and auspiciousness. At the very heart of this magnificent creation resides the Divine Mother. While our human eyes may perceive her as separate goddesses, the spiritual eye recognizes that these are but different facets of a single, boundless diamond. Maa Baglamukhi is the golden thread that runs through the center of this tapestry, intricately connected to every other expression of divine energy. When we stand before her, we are not merely standing before the Goddess of Stillness; we are standing before the sum of all divine perfections.

The Illuminating Insight: Mahāvidyā

Envision her first as **Mahāvidyā**—the ultimate source of primordial wisdom. This is the knowledge that does not come from books, but from the direct unraveling of the mysteries of existence. For the seeker struggling through the thickets of confusion, she is the sudden, sharp flash of insight that dispels the long night of the soul. In her Mahāvidyā aspect, she provides the profound understanding required to see through the grand illusion of the world.

The Wealth of the Soul: Mahālakṣmī

She is also **Mahālakṣmī**, yet we must look beyond the common pursuit of gold and material gain. While she provides prosperity as Mahālakṣmī, she is the bestower of a far greater treasure: the abundance of the spirit. She grants the true prosperity of inner peace, the wealth of well-being, and a spiritual richness that no thief can steal. Like a nurturing mother who ensures her children have all that is essential for a life of dignity, Baglamukhi ensures her devotees possess the 'inner currency' needed to navigate the world with grace. She fills the heart with a sense of 'enoughness,' transforming the poverty of the spirit into a radiant overflow of divine contentment.

The Radiant Harmony: Śrīmattripurasundarī

Furthermore, the Mother embodies **Śrīmattripurasundari**, the epitome of beauty, knowledge, and perfection, the exquisite goddess who reigns over the three worlds with absolute harmony. She is the epitome of divine grace, the enchanting allure that pulls every wandering soul back toward the source of pure consciousness.

Picture a lotus blossoming in the center of pristine, undisturbed waters; its petals radiate a serenity so profound that the mere sight of it stills the mind. This is the essence of Baglamukhi as Tripurasundari. She proves that true power is not ugly or harsh; it is breathtakingly beautiful. Her beauty is a weapon of light that captures the heart and dissolves the ego in a wave of sacred attraction.

The Cosmic Cradle: Bhuvaneśī and Jaganmātā

She is **Bhuvaneśī**, the Queen of the Spheres, the very mother of the universe who cradles all of creation within her infinite, loving embrace. As **Jaganmātā**, the Universal Mother, she does not merely rule over us from a distance; she sustains us. Every breath we take is a gift from her lungs; every pulse of life is a ripple of her heart. Just as a mother intuitively knows the needs of her child before they are even whispered, she sustains and protects all life, guiding the evolution of the cosmos with a wisdom that is as compassionate as it is vast. She is the space in which we live, move, and have our being.

The Bringer of All Good: Pārvatī and Sarvamangalā

And finally, she is **Pārvatī**, the mountain-born daughter who embodies the very essence of **Sarvamangalā**—the bringer of all that is auspicious, pure, and beneficial. Her presence is like a gentle, nutrient-rich rain that falls upon a parched earth, fostering growth, harmony, and well-being wherever it touches. In this form, she ensures that every action taken by the devotee leads toward a righteous end. She is the "Mangala" or the auspiciousness that turns a house into a home, a thought into a blessing, and a life into a sacred offering.

The Golden Synthesis: The Whole in the Part

Therefore, when we invoke Maa Baglamukhi, we must expand our vision. We are not calling upon a single, isolated deity. We are calling upon the combined majesty, the gathered power, and the unified grace of all the magnificent forms of the Divine Mother.

She is the ultimate synthesis—the source of wisdom, the bestower of prosperity, the epitome of beauty, the sustainer of worlds, and the embodiment of all that is good. She is the golden bridge that connects the fierce power of Stambhana with the gentle grace of Mā (Mother). By her mercy, the devotee finds a path that leads not just to the destruction of enemies, but to a life overflowing with enlightenment, abundance, and everlasting spiritual well-being.

VERSE 3

ललिता भैरवी शान्ता अन्नपूर्णा कुलेश्वरी ।
वाराही छीन्नमस्ता च तारा काली सरस्वती ॥ ३ ॥

Lalitā Bhairavī Śāntā Annapūrṇā Kuleśvarī ।
Vārāhī Chinnamastā Ca Tārā Kālī Sarasvatī ॥ 3 ॥

ललिता (अन्तर्मुखी रूप), भैरवी (क्रोध स्वरूपता), शांता (शांति स्वरूपता), अन्नपूर्णा (अन्न की देवी), कुलेश्वरी (कुल और परिवार की प्रभुता), वाराही (भगवान विष्णु की अवतारिणी), छिन्नमस्ता (भयानक रूप जो प्रत्येक समय प्रत्येक में अपने भक्तों के शत्रुओं को नष्ट करती हैं), तारा (संग्रह, शक्ति, और शांति की देवी), काली (समय/काल की देवी), और सरस्वती (विद्या, कला, और संवेदनशीलता की देवी) आप ही हैं

Lalita (introverted form), Bhairavi (anger form), Shanta (peace
form), Annapurna (goddess of food), Kuleshwari (dominion of clan
and family), Varahi (incarnation of Lord Vishnu), Chhinnamasta
(terrible form which appears every time You are the one who
destroys the enemies of your devotees.), Tara (goddess of collection,
power, and peace), Kali (goddess of time), and Saraswati (goddess of
learning, arts, and sensitivity)..

The Divine Mirror: Lalitā, Bhairavī, and Śāntā

Envision the Mother first as **Lalitā (Playful)**, the exquisitely beautiful and deeply introspective queen of the soul. In this facet, Baglamukhi represents the inward journey—the quiet, sacred path toward self-realization and the shimmering bliss of pure consciousness. Like a solitary lotus blooming in the silence of a hidden lake, this aspect guides us away from the noise of the world and into the serene depths of our own being, where the true self resides in eternal peace.

Yet, this gentle beauty possesses a fierce core, for she is also **Bhairavī**. She embodies the fiery, transformative power that acts as a divine furnace for the soul. Bhairavī is the flame that does not just warm, but consumes—burning away the dross of negativity, purification through the fire of truth. When the devotee faces internal demons or external threats, this facet of Baglamukhi rises with righteous, holy anger, providing the heat necessary to melt even the most stubborn obstacles.

And beneath the fire and the beauty lies **Śāntā**, the embodiment of profound, unshakeable peace. She is the "Still Point" at the center of the spinning world. Even when the storms of life rage with their greatest fury, the Śāntā aspect of Baglamukhi remains like a calm lake reflecting an endless sky. She bestows upon us the gift of equanimity, ensuring that our internal temple remains undisturbed by the chaos of the external world.

The Nurturer and the Protector: Annapūrṇā and Kuleśvarī

She manifests as Annapūrṇā, the Mother who ensures her children never hunger. And let's be honest—while we all certainly appreciate a well-stocked pantry, the soul often craves a far more complex menu. She serves the spiritual sustenance that feeds the starving heart. Like a golden harvest that never seems to run out, this facet of Baglamukhi ensures her devotees are provided with everything they truly need: physical sustenance, material stability, emotional comfort, and the essential 'daily bread' of divine inspiration.

As **Kuleśvarī**, she becomes the guardian of the roots. She is the protectress of the lineage, the family, and the sacred traditions that bind a community together. She acts as the heavy stone foundation of a magnificent temple; though she may be unseen, it is her strength that prevents the structure from crumbling. She ensures the continuity of our values and the safety of our homes, wrapping her protective arms around the very fabric of our social and familial bonds.

The Unwavering Warriors: Vārāhī and Chīnnamastā

Within the heart of Baglamukhi pulses the energy of **Vārāhī**, the powerful boar-headed goddess. Vārāhī represents absolute, unwavering determination of the Divine. She is the force that cannot be deterred, the divine plow that moves through the hardest earth to prepare for new growth. In this form, the Mother empowers us with a lion-hearted courage, granting us the ability to stand firm and overcome even the most formidable adversaries with a strength rooted in the earth itself.

Beside this strength sits the fierce grace of **Chīnnamastā**, the goddess who severs her own head to nourish her devotees. This is the ultimate symbol of the death of the ego—the realization that we must "lose our head" to find our spirit. Chīnnamastā is the power of absolute, selfless giving and the total transcendence of limited identity. When external or internal enemies threaten to paralyze us, this facet of Baglamukhi strikes with a lightning-fast, unwavering resolve, destroying the chains of the ego that keep us bound to fear.

The Saviors of the Spirit: Tārā, Kālī, and Sarasvatī

She embodies **Tārā**, the compassionate savior who hears the cries of those drowning in the ocean of existence. Like the North Star that remains fixed while all others move, this aspect of Baglamukhi offers a constant point of navigation. She provides the protection and strength needed to cross the "turbulent waters" of life's trials, guiding us through the darkness with the light of her mercy.

Then, there is the raw, primal power of **Kālī**, the goddess of Time and Transformation. Kālī is the dark earth from which all life springs and to which all life returns. She represents the dissolution of the old, the decaying, and the rigid, making space for a new and higher reality. This aspect of Baglamukhi helps the devotee to embrace the cycles of change, teaching us that every "end" is merely a prelude to a more magnificent beginning.

Finally, she encompasses **Sarasvatī**, the goddess of wisdom, art, and the sacred word. Like a flowing river of crystal-clear water, this facet of Baglamukhi blesses us with intellect, creativity, and the power of eloquence. She is the one who turns our speech into a weapon of truth and our thoughts into a work of art. She provides the "Vak" (speech) that is controlled and potent, ensuring that when we speak, our words have the weight of divine authority.

The Radiant Confluence: The Whole Mahāvidyā Path

Therefore, we must see that Maa Baglamukhi is not a singular, isolated entity, but a radiant synthesis of all the Great Wisdom Goddesses. She is a spiritual prism that holds the introverted peace of Lalitā, the purifying fire of Bhairavī, the tranquil silence of Śāntā, and the nourishing grace of Annapūrṇā. She carries the protective shield of Kuleśvarī, the iron will of Vārāhī, the ego-shattering resolve of Chīnnamastā, the guiding light of Tārā, the transformative depth of Kālī, and the illuminating brilliance of Saraswati.

By stepping into the golden aura of Maa Baglamukhi, we gain access to the treasury of all other Mahavidyas. We are not just worshipping a goddess; we are engaging with the totality of the Divine Feminine, empowered on every level of our being—physical, mental, and eternal.

VERSE 4

जगत्पूज्या महामाया कामेशी भगमालिनी ।
दक्षपुत्री शिवांकस्था शिवरुपा शिवप्रिया ॥ ४ ॥

Jagatpūjyā Mahāmāyā Kāmeśī Bhagamālinī ।
Dakṣaputrī Śivānkasthā Śivarupā Śivapriyā ॥ 4 ॥

पूर्ण जगत द्वारा पूजे जानी वाली, महामाया, कामेशी (इच्छाओं और कामनाओं की अधिपति), भगमालिनी (समस्त सृष्टि की नियंत्रण करने वाली और सभी प्रकार के भोगों की देवी), दक्ष की पुत्री (देवी सती), शिवांकस्था (शिव की अर्धांगिनी), आप शिव का रूप हैं (शिव की आध्यात्मिक और दिव्य शक्ति), शिव प्रिया हैं।

Worshiped by the entire world, Mahamaya, Kameshi (lord of desires and wishes), Bhagmalini (controller of the entire creation and goddess of all kinds of enjoyments), daughter of Daksha (Goddess Sati), Shivankastha (consort of Shiva), You are the form of Shiva (spiritual and divine power of Shiva), You are Shiva-Priya..

The Object of Universal Adoration: Jagatpūjyā and Mahāmāyā

Imagine the entire cosmos—from the smallest atom to the most distant galaxy—bowing in silent reverence. Maa Baglamukhi is **Jagatpūjyā,** the one whose feet are worshipped by every world and every dimension. She is the universal sanctuary. Yet, she is also **Mahāmāyā,** the Great Weaver of Illusion. As Mahāmāyā, she is the very fabric of the reality we touch and see, a tapestry woven from the threads of divine consciousness. She is the paradox: she is the power that veils the ultimate truth with the "play" of the world, yet she is also the only one who can lift that veil. Within this vast cloak of Mahāmāyā lies the 'smoky' essence of **Dhūmāvatī;** she is the one who first shows us the transience of the world—like smoke—before Baglamukhi's stillness dissolves the illusion entirely.

Ultimately, she is one of the ten Mahāvidyās, representing the oldest and most misunderstood aspect of the Divine Mother—the void that remains when all else dissolves. She is The Smoky Widow, representing the profound wisdom found in solitude and disappointment, teaching us that when worldly expectations crumble, only the truth remains. Her story is often interpreted esoterically, not as a literal event, but as a metaphor for the Divine Mother consuming the entire universe (represented by Shiva) and the "smoke" representing the state of the world—transient and illusory—that remains before total dissolution. Like a master magician who conjures a breathtaking spectacle, she orchestrates the cosmic dance of creation, preservation, and dissolution. To worship her is to ask the magician to show us what lies behind the curtain of the material world.

The Sovereign of Longing: Kāmeśī and Bhagamālinī

She is **Kāmeśī,** the sovereign of all desires and wishes. She holds the reins of the human heart's longing. This is not a force that encourages mere worldly indulgence; rather, it is the divine impulse that drives the soul toward its true purpose. Think of the inherent yearning of a seed buried in the dark earth, pushing upward toward the sun—Kāmeśī is that nurturing energy, the holy desire for growth and ultimate union with the Source.

Within her also resides the essence of **Bhagamālinī**, the one who wears the flowering garlands of creation's joys. She is the controller of the cosmic garden and the bestower of all enjoyments. However, the "pleasures" she grants are the profound bliss of spiritual realization and the harmony of a life lived in alignment with the Divine. Like a skilled gardener who ensures every blossom is nourished, she governs the cosmic order to ensure that the joy of the soul eventually flowers into its full radiance. Together, these aspects of the Mother transform our erratic cravings into intentional prayer, turning the chaotic pursuit of 'more' into the elegant fulfillment of 'becoming.' By embracing both the yearning and the blossoming, we find that our deepest desires are not distractions, but the very compass points guiding us home.

The Sacred Lineage: Dakṣaputrī

The Mother is recognized as **Dakṣaputrī**, the daughter of Daksha. This title carries the weight of a fierce and ancient history, linking her to the narrative of Sati and her unwavering, sacrificial devotion. This lineage underscores her role as the primordial **Shakti**. It speaks of her fierce loyalty to the Truth and her identity as the original feminine power that exists before time began. She is the daughter of the earth's tradition, yet she is the one who transcends it with her divine fire.

In the context of Baglamukhi Sadhana, being 'Dakshaputri' signifies that a seeker must respect their 'roots' and 'conditioning' while identifying the ego hidden within them. Just as Maa destroyed Daksha's ego to choose Shiva (Pure Consciousness), this form inspires us to break free from our mental rigidities and move toward supreme awareness.

The Inseparable Oneness: Śivānkasthā and Śivarupā

The most profound mystery of this verse lies in her relationship with the Divine Masculine. She is **Śivānkasthā**, the one who resides on the lap of Shiva. This is a symbol of the absolute, inseparable union of Energy (Shakti) and Consciousness (Shiva). It is the dynamic interplay that forms the very foundation of existence.

Picture the Ardhanarishvara—the form that is half-man and half-woman—where the boundary between the two dissolves. Maa Baglamukhi is the embodiment of this oneness. She is also **Śivarupā**, the very form of Shiva himself. This tells us that at the highest level, there is no difference between the power and the one who wields it. Just as fire cannot be separated from its heat, or the sun from its light, Baglamukhi embodies both the dynamic, "stopping" energy of Shakti and the silent, witnessing awareness of Shiva. She is the feminine face of the Infinite.

The Eternal Beloved: Śivapriyā

Finally, she is **Śivapriyā**, the beloved of Shiva. This title signifies the deep, eternal bond of love that keeps the universe in balance. It is a connection of harmony and essential necessity. In the cosmic dance, she is the rhythm to his melody, the strength to his stillness. Their relationship is the ultimate archetype of love—a bond that is not based on need, but on the blissful recognition of each other's divinity.

The Universal Sovereign

Therefore, Maa Baglamukhi stands as the universally worshipped **Mahāmāyā**, the sovereign over our deepest yearnings, the governor of cosmic joy, the royal daughter of the sacred lineage, and the inseparable beloved of the Great Lord. She is the supreme expression of the Divine Feminine, whose grace is sought by gods and mortals alike. By her power, the illusions of the world are stilled, and the devotee is led—through desire, through devotion, and through wisdom—to the ultimate union, where the soul finally finds its rest in the lap of the Divine.

VERSE 5

सर्व-सम्पत्करी देवी सर्वलोक वशंकरी ।
वेदविद्या महापूज्या भक्ताद्वेषी भयंकरी ॥ ५ ॥

Sarva-Sampatkarī Devī Sarvaloka Vaśankarī ।
Vedavidyā Mahāpūjyā Bhaktādveṣī Bhayankarī ॥ 5 ॥

सभी को ऐश्वर्य, समृद्धियाँ देने वाली, सभी लोकों को वश में करने वाली, आप वेदों और विद्या की महान पूज्यनीय हैं (ज्ञान की देवी), और अपने भक्तों से द्वेष करने वालों (दुष्टों) के लिए भयंकर रूप धारण करती हैं।

The giver of opulence and prosperity to all, the one who subdues all the worlds, you are the great worshiper of the Vedas and Vidya (goddess of knowledge), and assume a terrible form for those who hate your devotees (evildoers)..

The Queen of Infinite Opulence: Sarva-Sampatkarī

Imagine a queen whose heart is as vast as the universe she governs, a sovereign whose greatest joy is the prosperity of her subjects. Maa Baglamukhi is **Sarva-Sampatkarī Devī**—the Goddess who is the architect and bestower of all forms of wealth. When we call upon her in this aspect, we are not just asking for coins or comfort. We are invoking the source of "Sampatti"—the true opulence that includes spiritual depth, physical health, clarity of mind, and the fulfillment of the soul's deepest needs.

Think of a celestial wish-fulfilling tree (Kalpavriksha), its branches heavy with the golden fruits of every noble desire. Whether it is the material stability needed to live with dignity or the spiritual riches needed to attain liberation, she is the one who provides. She reminds us that abundance is our birthright when we align ourselves with the Divine Flow.

The Sovereign of Cosmic Balance: Sarvaloka Vaśankarī

Her influence extends far beyond the reach of human eyes, encompassing the very fabric of every dimension. She is **Sarvaloka Vaśankarī**, the one who subdues and harmonizes all the worlds. This "subduing" is not born of a tyrant's force, but of an inherent, irresistible divine authority. It is the power of Truth itself.

Like a master diplomat who restores order to a world in chaos, Maa Baglamukhi establishes a perfect equilibrium among the cosmic forces. She "charms" the universe back into alignment with divine law. When we feel that the world around us is spinning out of control, we look to her as the central axis of power, the one who can still the waves of universal unrest and bring all of creation into a state of sacred order.

The Heart of Sacred Wisdom: Vedavidyā and Mahāpūjyā

Within the silent depths of the Mother resides the profound wisdom enshrined in the Vedas and all sacred scriptures. She is **Vedavidyā** and **Mahāpūjyā**—the greatly revered embodiment of divine knowledge. She is not just a protector of the texts; she is the essence of the wisdom they contain.

Picture a sage who has spent a thousand years in deep meditation, becoming so one with the Truth that they radiate light; this is the energy Baglamukhi holds. She is the illuminating light that makes the complex simple and the hidden visible. To worship her as Vedavidyā is to seek the highest education of the soul, the insight that allows us to read the book of the universe with the eyes of an awakened being.

The Fierce Shield of the Soul: Bhaktādveṣī and Bhayankarī

However, this benevolent queen and wise teacher possesses another side—a side born of an unwavering, fierce compassion. For those who harbor malice, hatred, or ill-will toward her devotees, she becomes **Bhaktādveṣī and Bhayankarī**. In this moment, she assumes a form so terrifying that the very hearts of the wicked are frozen with fear.

Imagine a mother whose child is suddenly threatened. In an instant, her tenderness vanishes, replaced by a primal, unstoppable protective fury. Maa Baglamukhi stands as an impenetrable shield for her "beloved children." Her terrifying aspect is not a sign of cruelty, but a manifestation of her absolute commitment to Justice. For a dark force attempting to harm a pure soul, her presence is the "Stambhana"—the paralyzing strike that dismantles the intentions of the unjust. She proves that to be truly compassionate, one must also be willing to be a fierce warrior against the forces of negativity.

The Golden Synthesis of Peace and Power

Therefore, we see Maa Baglamukhi as the ultimate guardian of our lives. She is the compassionate mother who showers us with the "Sampatti" of well-being, the sovereign who keeps the universe in check, and the sage who whispers the secrets of the Vedas into our hearts.

Yet, she is also the formidable guardian who stands at the gate of our spiritual journey, ready to strike terror into anything that seeks to harm our progress. In her, we find the perfect balance: the generosity that gives us everything we need to grow, and the fierce protection that ensures we have the safety to do so. She is the golden wall between her devotees and the shadows of the world, ensuring that righteousness always has the final word.

VERSE 6

स्तम्भ-रुपा स्तम्भिनी च दुष्टस्तम्भनकारिणी ।
भक्तप्रिया महाभोगा श्रीविद्या ललिताम्बिका ॥ ६ ॥

Stambha-Rupā Stambhinī Ca Duṣṭastambhanakāriṇī ।
Bhaktapriyā Mahābhogā Śrīvidyā Lalitāmbikā ॥ 6 ॥

आप स्तंभरूपा (स्थिरता और अचलता का प्रतीक) हैं जो संकट के समय में अपने भक्तों को दृढ़ता प्रदान करती हैं। आप स्तंभित करने की शक्ति हैं जो दुष्टों की नकारात्मक शक्तियों और क्रियाओं को रोकने में सक्षम है। आप दुष्टों को स्तंभित करने की कारक हैं, भक्तों की प्रिय हैं, महा सुख प्रदान करती हैं, आप ही श्रीविद्या लक्ष्मी हैं और ललिताम्बिका हैं जो सौंदर्य, समृद्धि, और दिव्य ज्ञान की देवी हैं।

You are the pillar (symbol of stability and immovability) who provides strength to your devotees in times of crisis. You are the power to erect that is able to stop the negative forces and actions of the wicked. You are the destroyer of the wicked, beloved of the devotees, the giver of great happiness, you are Srividya Lakshmi and Lalitambika, the goddess of beauty, prosperity, and divine knowledge..

The Unshakeable Axis: Stambha-Rupā

Imagine a fierce and mindless storm raging across the landscape of your life, threatening to uproot your peace, your family, and your very purpose. In this moment of terrifying chaos, Maa Baglamukhi manifests as **Stambha-Rupā**—the unshakeable pillar. She is the very embodiment of stability and immovability.

Like a mountain whose roots reach into the very heart of the earth, she stands unshaken when the storms of life begin to howl. For the devotee, she becomes the ultimate anchor. When the world feels like it is spinning out of control, she is the fixed point of strength that you can lean upon. Her presence says, "I am here, and I will not move.' She provides the unwavering support that allows us to stand tall even when the earth beneath us seems to tremble.

The Divine Paralysis: Stambhini and Duṣṭastambhanakāriṇī

Beyond being a pillar herself, she is **Stambhini**—the active power that paralyzes and renders ineffective the malicious forces of the wicked. Picture a venomous snake, coiled and poised to strike with deadly intent, suddenly frozen into a statue by a single golden glance. This is the "Stambhana" power in action. She does not always choose to destroy the enemy; often, she simply neutralizes their ability to harm.

As **Duṣṭastambhanakāriṇī**, she is the definitive cause of this immobilization. Her divine will acts as an impenetrable, invisible barrier. She silences the harmful voices that spread slander and halts the destructive plans before they can even begin to manifest. Think of it as a holy spell that binds the hands of evil, preventing it from casting a shadow upon the innocent. She wields this power with a righteous and focused intent, proving that the greatest weapon is often the one that creates absolute silence. This divine silence is not merely a void, but a sacred pause that allows our own inner clarity to surface, unburdened by the chaos of the world. By invoking her, we learn that true strength lies not in shouting back at the noise, but in the power to command stillness within ourselves and our surroundings.

The Lioness and Her Cubs: Bhaktapriya

Yet, we must never mistake this formidable power for coldness. Amidst the "iron" of her paralysis, she remains **Bhaktapriya**—the one who is deeply beloved by her devotees and who, in turn, loves them with infinite intensity.

Her strength is a refuge, a sanctuary of profound love and understanding. Imagine a fierce lioness, her claws and teeth ready for battle, yet her touch is incredibly tender as she grooms and protects her cubs. This is the nature of Baglamukhi's love. She is fierce to the world so that she can be soft to you. She is the protector who knows your heart's whispers and values your devotion above all else.

The Source of Infinite Joy: Mahābhoga

She is also the giver of **Mahābhoga**, the bestower of the "Great Enjoyment." This is not limited to the fleeting, shallow pleasures of the senses that leave us feeling empty. "Mahābhoga" refers to a profound, transcendent joy that arises from spiritual evolution and a deep connection to the Divine.

Picture a soul that has finally stopped "chasing" and has begun "resting" in divine grace. This is the deep satisfaction and bliss that Baglamukhi provides. She ensures that her devotees experience the fullness of life, where every breath is infused with the sweetness of her presence. She is the source of a happiness so deep that it cannot be shaken by external gain or loss.

The Radiant Wisdom: Śrīvidyā and Lalitāmbikā

Furthermore, she is **Śrīvidyā**, the embodiment of the most sacred and secret knowledge. This is the "Lakshmi" of the intellect—the wisdom that leads to both material success and spiritual liberation. Like a radiant, multi-faceted gem that bestows both physical beauty and immense wealth, this aspect of the Mother grants us the discernment to live a life of abundance without losing our way.

Finally, she reveals herself as **Lalitāmbikā**, the Beautiful and Graceful Mother of the Universe. She is the epitome of elegance, prosperity, and divine knowledge. Imagine a goddess whose radiant presence fills the entire cosmos with a golden light that tastes like honey and feels like home. This is the all-encompassing grace of Maa Baglamukhi. She is the proof that the ultimate power of the universe is not just strong, but breathtakingly beautiful and infinitely kind.

The Golden Synthesis

Therefore, we see Maa Baglamukhi as the unshakeable pillar in our moments of weakness, the silent paralyzer of our enemies, and the loving guardian of our souls. She is the source of our highest joys and the teacher of our deepest wisdom. To walk her path is to be anchored in strength, protected by her fierce love, and illuminated by her radiant beauty. She is the mother who stills the storm so that her child can finally know the peace of the dawn.

VERSE 7

मैनापुत्री शिवानन्दा मातंगी भुवनेश्वरी ।
नारसिंही नरेन्द्रा च नृपाराध्या नरोत्तमा ॥ ७ ॥

Maināputrī Śivānandā Mātangī Bhuvaneśvarī I
Nārasiṃhī Narendrā Ca Nṛpārādhyā Narottamā II 7 II

मैना की पुत्री (देवी पार्वती) हैं, शिवानंद (शिव की आराध्या और जीवन संगिनी) हैं, मातंगी (ज्ञान, संगीत, और वाक् शक्ति की देवी), भुवनेश्वरी (संपूर्ण ब्रह्मांड और सृष्टि की अधिष्ठात्री देवी) हैं, नारसिंही (भगवान नृसिंह की शक्ति) और नरेंद्रा (दिव्य संरक्षण और शासन) हैं। आप नृपाराध्या (राजाओं द्वारा पूजनीय), 'नरोत्तमा' (उत्कृष्ट मानवों में श्रेष्ठ, जो उनके दिव्य गुणों और आध्यात्मिक उत्कर्ष को संदर्भित करता है) है।

You are the daughter of Maina (Goddess Parvati), Shivananda (worshipper and life partner of Shiva), Matangi (goddess of knowledge, music, and speech), Bhuvaneshwari (presiding goddess of the entire universe and creation), Narasimhi (Lord Narsimha). power) and Narendra (divine protection and rule). You are Nriparadhya (revered by kings), 'Narottama' (best among exalted human beings, which refers to their divine qualities and spiritual exaltation)..

The Serene Strength of the Heights: Maināputrī and Śivānandā

Imagine the majestic Himalayas, those silent, white guardians of the world where the air is thin and the spirit is thick with power. From the heart of these towering peaks emerged Maināputrī, the daughter of Queen Maina—the beloved Parvati herself. In this aspect, Maa Baglamukhi embodies the serene, unshakable strength of the mountains. She is the divine feminine rooted in steadfastness, a presence so absolute that it brings the wildest storms of the mind to a perfect, silent stillness.

She is also **Śivānandā**, the one who exists in a state of perpetual bliss through her union with Lord Shiva. This is the eternal dance of consciousness and energy, where the individual drop of water realizes it has always been the ocean. Like the perfect harmony between two souls whose love is so pure that it sustains the universe, Maa Baglamukhi and Shiva represent the ultimate union. Her presence brings the "Ananda" (bliss) of Shiva into our lives, reminding us that the end of all spiritual struggle is a state of profound, ecstatic joy.

The Voice of the Soul and the Cosmic Queen: Mātangī and Bhuvaneśvarī

Envision the vibrant energy of knowledge, music, and speech flowing through the cosmos like a golden river. Maa Baglamukhi embodies **Mātangī**, the goddess of the "spoken word" and the fine arts. Like a master musician whose melodies can melt a heart of stone, or a wise poet whose words can ignite a revolution of the spirit, this aspect of the Mother bestows eloquence and artistic genius. She is the one who puts the power of "Vak" (speech) into our mouths, ensuring that our words are not just noise, but instruments of divine truth and beauty.

She expands further to become **Bhuvaneśvarī**, the Queen of the Universe and the presiding deity of all that is manifest. Like a loving mother who governs her household with a mixture of firm wisdom and tender compassion, she oversees the vast, sprawling expanse of the cosmos. She is the space in which we breathe and the womb in which all creation is nurtured. Under her gaze, nothing is lost and no one is forgotten; she cradles every being within her infinite, protective embrace.

The Fierce Guardian and the Divine Ruler: Nārasiṃhī and Narendrā

Within her golden form resides the lightning-fast energy of **Nārasiṃhī**, the feminine power of Lord Narasimha. This is the lion-headed energy of Vishnu, the fierce protector who manifests in a heartbeat to vanquish evil and defend the innocent. When a pure soul is threatened, Baglamukhi as Nārasiṃhī rises with a roar that shakes the three worlds. She is the swift justice that strikes down the tyrant and the "impulse of protection" that keeps the devotee safe from the shadows of injustice.

She is also **Narendrā**, the ruler among humans, signifying that all just governance is a reflection of her divine authority. She is the grace that sits upon the brow of a wise and benevolent leader. Like a king who ensures the well-being of the lowliest citizen, Maa Baglamukhi bestows her wisdom upon those in positions of power, guiding them to rule with a heart of Dharma. She reminds us that true leadership is a sacred service for the souls under one's care.

The Excellence of the Human Spirit: Nṛpārādhyā and Narottamā

As **Nṛpārādhyā**, she is the one revered by kings and emperors. Imagine the most powerful monarchs of history, their crowns laid at her feet, bowing in humble devotion to seek the guidance needed to lead a prosperous nation. They recognize that their worldly power is a mere loan from her infinite treasury. She is the source of the strategic wisdom and the moral courage required to hold a scepter.

Finally, she is **Narottamā**, the very best among human beings—the embodiment of the highest potential of our evolution. She represents the "Exalted One" who has attained spiritual perfection. Like a beacon of pure light standing at the end of a long journey, this aspect of the Mother inspires us to strive for inner excellence. She shows us that the goal of life is to become "Narottama"—to manifest the divine qualities of the Goddess within our own human form.

The Golden Synthesis of Grace and Governance

Therefore, Maa Baglamukhi is the serene mountain-strength of Parvati, the blissful partner of the Infinite, the eloquent voice of Mātangī, and the cosmic mother Bhuvaneśvarī. She carries the fierce lion-heart of Nārasiṃhī, the royal authority of Narendrā, and the spiritual perfection of Narottamā.

She encompasses the Divine Feminine in its most nurturing and its most commanding forms. To worship her is to seek not only protection, but also the inspiration to grow into the most excellent version of ourselves. She is the mother who protects the world, the queen who guides our actions, and the light that leads us toward the peak of our own spiritual evolution.

VERSE 8

नागिनी नागपुत्री च नगराजसुता उमा ।
पीताम्बा पीतपुष्पा च पीतवस्त्रप्रिया शुभा ॥ ८ ॥

Nāginī Nāgaputrī Ca Nagarājasutā Umā ।
Pītāmbā Pītapuṣpā Ca Pītavastrapriyā Śubhā ॥ 8 ॥

आप नागिनी नाग की पुत्री हैं, नगराज (नागो के राजा) की पुत्री हैं जिनका नाम उमा है। आप पीले रंग के वस्त्र प्रिय हैं, आप को पीले पुष्प प्रिय हैं, आप शुभता और कल्याणकारी हैं।

You are the daughter of Nagini Naag, daughter of Nagaraj (The king of snakes) whose name is Uma. You love yellow clothes, you love yellow flowers, you are auspicious..

The Wisdom of the Deep: Nāginī and Nāgaputrī

Imagine descending into the mystical, shimmering realm of the **Nagas**—the serpent deities who, in our ancient traditions, are the guardians of the earth's deepest treasures and the keepers of hidden wisdom. Maa Baglamukhi is revered as **Nāginī** and **Nāgaputrī**, the daughter of the serpent queen.

This is a connection of immense spiritual significance. The serpent represents the Kundalini energy, the potent and coiled power that resides within us all. By embodying this lineage, the Mother signals her absolute mastery over these hidden currents of life. She is the one who can navigate the dark, winding tunnels of our subconscious, offering protection against the "venom" of unseen dangers—those secret enemies and hidden anxieties that strike from the shadows. To worship her in this form is to seek the wisdom that lies beneath the surface of reality.

The Mountain Queen and the Serpent King: Nagarājasutā Umā

She is the cherished daughter of **Nagaraj**, the King of the serpents, the one who supports the very foundations of the world. As **Nagarājasutā Umā**, she stands as a bridge between the deep earth and the high heavens. Here, the name **Umā** connects her directly to the heart of Goddess Parvati, the eternal consort of Shiva.

In this facet, she is the embodiment of raw power, fertility, and unshakeable protection. Just as the serpent king provides stability to the ground we walk upon, the Mother as Umā provides a spiritual foundation for our lives. She is the daughter of the heights and the depths, a protector whose loyalty to her devotees is as enduring as the mountains and as deep as the primordial waters.

The Radiance of the Sun: Pītāmbā

Envision a vast field, stretching as far as the eye can see, bathed in the liquid gold of the midday sun. Maa Baglamukhi is **Pītāmbā**, the one whose very being is draped in yellow. In our sacred tradition, yellow is not just a color; it is a frequency of purity, auspiciousness, and the "Tejas" (radiant energy) of the sun.

Her golden robes are more than attire—they are a manifestation of her illuminating power. They represent her ability to act as a cosmic lamp, piercing through the thickest darkness of depression, doubt, and negativity. When she wraps her golden aura around a devotee, the shadows of misfortune simply cease to exist, dissolved by the sheer intensity of her light.

The Offering of the Heart: Pītapuṣpā

She takes immense delight in Pītapuṣpā—the yellow flowers that are offered to her with a pure heart. These vibrant blossoms, whether they be marigolds or turmeric-stained petals, symbolize the "flowering" of our own lives.

However, the esoteric essence of this offering runs much deeper than the physical bloom. In the alchemy of the Divine Mother, the color yellow also represents the frequency of wisdom, clarity, and the dissolution of the ego's sharp edges. Therefore, the true Pītapuṣpā is not merely gathered from a garden; it is plucked from the landscape of the subconscious. To offer "yellow" to the Mother is to perform a sacred act of surrender—it is to pluck the heavy, withered petals of our long-held grudges, the sharp thorns of enmity, and the bitter roots of resentment from the garden of our spirit.

These are the "real" flowers. When a seeker offers these to the Mother, they are essentially declaring, "I relinquish the toxicity of hatred so that I may receive the nectar of your clarity."

Imagine a seeker offering a bouquet of golden blooms with heartfelt reverence; this act is a symbol of the blossoming of prosperity and spiritual growth within the soul, nourished by the soil of a cleansed heart. The Mother receives these offerings—both the physical flower and the internal surrender—with a grace that is as warm as the color she loves. She multiplies our surrender, returning it to us as a life overflowing with auspiciousness, peace, and the radiant sunshine of her divine presence.

The Essence of All Good: Pītavastrapriyā Śubhā

Finally, she is **Pītavastrapriyā Śubhā**, the one who truly loves the yellow cloth and is the very essence of **Shubha** (auspiciousness). This love for yellow emphasizes her connection to everything that is beneficial, pure, and life-affirming.

Her presence in a home or a heart acts as a divine filter, dispelling "Ashubha" (misfortune) and ushering in positive, constructive energies. She is the auspiciousness that makes a task successful and a journey safe. She is the golden glow that remains when the storms of life have passed, ensuring that her devotees walk in a light that never fades.

The Golden Guardian of Earth and Sky

Therefore, Maa Baglamukhi stands as the mystic daughter of the Nagas, the embodiment of Kundalini, the steadfast princess Umā, and the radiant Queen of Gold. She is the internal compass guiding us through the hidden realms of our own minds, providing the unwavering support that elevates our spirit toward the light.

She is the master of the 'yellow ray'—that potent energy that heals, protects, and enlightens. By her grace, the hidden dangers of the world are neutralized, and our lives are transformed into a vibrant field of golden flowers, blooming under the watchful and loving eyes of the Mother.

VERSE 9

पीतगन्धप्रिया रामा पीतरत्नार्चिता शिवा ।
अर्द्धचन्द्रघरी देवी गदामुद्गरधारिणी ॥ ९ ॥

Pītagandhapriyā Rāmā Pītaratnārcitā Śivā |
Arddhacandradharī Devī Gadāmudgaradhāriṇī || 9 ||

आपको पीला चंदन प्रिय है, रामा (धर्म का पालन करने वाली) है, आप ही शिवा हैं जिन्हें पीले रत्न अर्चित किए जाते हैं। आप देवी ने अर्ध-चन्द्र (मुख) धारण किया है जो सौंदर्यपूर्ण और शान्त है, आपने गदा और मुद्गर धारण किया है।

You love yellow aroma, you are Rama (follower of religion), you are Shiva to whom yellow gems are offered. You goddess is wearing a half-moon (face) which is beautiful and peaceful, you are wearing a mace and a club..

The Earthly Aroma of Devotion: Pītagandhapriyā

Imagine entering a sanctified space where the air is thick and sweet with the scent of golden sandalwood. Maa Baglamukhi is **Pītagandhapriyā**, the one who delights in this yellow fragrance. In our path, sandalwood is not just a perfume; it is a symbol of the cooling, grounding energy of the earth.

When a devotee anoints her image with a yellow tilak, it is a profound gesture of seeking stability. The fragrance represents the "scent of virtue" that should emanate from a seeker's life. By offering what she loves, we are asking the Mother to cool the fires of our anxiety and to ground our restless minds in the fertile soil of her presence. She reminds us that true devotion is a multisensory experience—a fragrance that lingers in the soul long after the ritual is done.

The Standard of Righteousness and Radiance: Rāmā

She is also revered as **Rāmā,** a name that vibrates with the energy of absolute righteousness and the upholding of Dharma. Just as the avatar Lord Rama stood as the "Maryada Purushottama"—the supreme practitioner of ethics—Maa Baglamukhi as Rāmā becomes our internal moral compass. She is the one who ensures that our victories are not just successful, but just. She guides her devotees along the narrow and difficult path of moral strength, ensuring that even as we seek to "still" the distractions and enemies within, we remain aligned with the highest principles of Truth.

However, the name Rāmā holds a deeper, more golden resonance. In the ancient lexicon of the Divine, the elongated sound of "Rāmā" is a sacred epithet for Goddess Lakshmi herself—the embodiment of abundance, beauty, and the flowing grace of the universe.

This is the divine synthesis that Maa Baglamukhi invites us to master. She teaches us that Dharma (the law of righteousness) and Dhana (the flow of abundance) are not two different paths; they are the two lungs of a spiritual life.

The "Rama" Aspect: Provides the structure, the backbone, and the integrity. It is the wisdom to know what is right.

The "Rāmā" Aspect: Provides the fruit, the beauty, and the prosperity. It is the grace that manifests when we live in alignment with that truth.

Too often, seekers make the mistake of chasing the "Rāmā" (abundance) while ignoring the "Rama" (the rules of the game). They want the gold without the integrity. Maa Baglamukhi, in her infinite, sometimes jarring, wisdom, stands at the crossroads of both. She uses her power of Stambhan (stillness) to halt our desperate, ego-driven chase for wealth, forcing us to pause and realign with Dharma.

She reminds us: "Seek the Righteousness first, and the Radiance will follow." To worship her as Rāmā is to make a vow that our power will never be used for the petty sake of the ego, but for the expansion of the Right. When we align our internal moral compass with hers, we find that the "stillness" she provides is not empty—it is the fertile soil where true, sustainable prosperity is finally allowed to grow.

The Jewel of Consciousness: Pītaratnārcitā and Śivā

Envision the radiant glow of precious yellow topazes and golden sapphires offered at her feet, their brilliance mirroring her own divine effulgence. She is **Pītaratnārcitā**—the auspicious one who is worshipped with these golden jewels.

But these gems are more than mere stones; they represent the "jewels of the mind"—our most valued qualities of clarity, focus, and devotion. When we offer these to her, we are recognizing her supreme sovereignty over our inner world. She is **"Śivā,"** the feminine essence of the divine power of Shiva, indicating that within her golden form resides the same transformative capacity to dissolve the universe and rebuild it in light.

The Moon of Tranquility: Arddhacandradharī Devī

Her divine aspect is a study in serene beauty, adorned with the gentle, silver curve of the **Arddhacandradharī Devī**—the goddess who wears the crescent moon. This moon, resting upon her forehead, symbolizes the cooling of the intellect and the cyclical nature of time.

It is a gentle illumination that dispels the darkness of the night without the harshness of a scorching sun. It represents the "Amrita" (nectar) of immortality that drips from the moon of consciousness. Picture the soft, silver-gold glow gracing her brow; it tells the devotee that no matter how fierce the battle may seem, the Mother herself remains in a state of eternal peace and serenity.

The Hammer of Truth: Gadāmudgaradhāriṇī

Yet, do not let that moon-like peace fool you into thinking she is passive. When the situation demands it, she reveals herself as **Gadāmudgaradhāriṇī**—the bearer of the heavy mace and the club. These are not merely weapons; they are the tangible symbols of her authority to crush negativity.

The mace embodies the immovable weight of divine law, while the club is the precise instrument that silences falsehood at its source. Imagine her wielding these with a focused, righteous intensity. She does not strike to harm, but to protect; she strikes to dismantle the obstacles that block the devotee's progress toward the light. She is the warrior who ensures that when truth finally speaks, the noise of the world is silenced by the resonance of her golden power.

The Balance of Grace and Might

Therefore, Maa Baglamukhi is the lover of the sacred fragrance, the upholder of the moral law, the auspicious power worshipped with the mind's finest jewels, and the serene queen of the crescent moon.

But she is also the formidable guardian who stands ready with her mace.

She offers us the "sandalwood" of peace to calm our hearts and the "mace" of power to clear our paths. In her, the gentle grace of the moon and the heavy justice of the club exist in perfect harmony, offering every seeker a way to live with righteousness, to breathe in the fragrance of the divine, and to walk without fear in a world of shadows.

VERSE 10

सावित्री त्रिपदा शुद्धा सद्योराग विवर्धिनी ।
विष्णुरुपा जगन्मोहा ब्रह्मरुपा हरिप्रिया ॥ १० ॥

Sāvitrī Tripadā Śuddhā Sadyorāga Vivardhinī |
Viṣṇurupā Jaganmohā Brahmarupā Haripriyā ॥ 10 ॥

आप ही सावित्री हैं, त्रिपदा (गायत्री) हैं - जिनके तीन चरणों में सत्, रज, तम व्याप्त है, आप परम पवित्र हैं, आप सद्यों में ही रोगों को नष्ट करने वाली हैं और विवर्धन के साधने की देवी हैं॥ आप ही विष्णु का रूप हैं जो जगत को मोह लेता हैं, आप ही ब्रह्म रूप हैं, हरि (सृष्टि के पालनकर्ता और जीवन के संरक्षक) को प्रिया हैं।

You are Savitri, Tripada (Gayatri) - in whose three feet Sat, Raja, Tama are prevalent, you are the most pure, you are the one who destroys diseases in the Sadya itself and is the goddess of development. You are the form of Vishnu who fascinates the world, you are the form of Brahma, dear to Hari (the sustainer of creation and preserver of life)..

The Dawn of Consciousness: Sāvitrī

Imagine the world in that sacred, breathless moment just before dawn. As the first rays of the sun pierce the horizon, bathing the earth in liquid gold, we meet **Sāvitrī**. Maa Baglamukhi is the embodiment of this radiant solar energy—the primordial source of life and vitality.

Just as the physical sun dispels the literal darkness of the night and nourishes every blade of grass, the Mother as Sāvitrī dispels the inner darkness of our confusion. She is the "Life-Force" that wakes up our sleeping spirits. When we invoke her, we are asking for that morning sun to rise within our hearts, bringing with it the clarity, warmth, and sustenance required to face a new day of spiritual evolution.

The Sacred Rhythm of Existence: Tripadā

She is also **Tripada**, a name that resonates with the power of the holy Gayatri mantra. Her three "steps" or feet symbolize her sovereignty over the three realms—the Earth, the Atmosphere, and the Heavens. But more deeply, she represents the mastery over the three Gunas that compose all of nature: Sattva (purity), Rajas (passion), and Tamas (inertia).

Like just as the chanting of a mantra brings our breath into harmony with the universe, so does the Mother, in her form as Tripada (The Three-Footed One), balance these energies within us. She ensures that our passion remains infused with purity, and that our rest never descends into lethargy. She is the mathematical perfection of the universe, ensuring that from our physical bodies to the celestial realms—encompassing the three states of consciousness—everything exists in perfect harmony.

The Crystal Stream: Śuddhā and Sadyorāga Vivardhinī

Envision a pristine mountain stream, its waters so crystal clear and untouched that they seem to be made of liquid light. Maa

Baglamukhi is **Śuddhā**, the supremely pure one. She is free from any blemish, any shadow, or any ulterior motive. Her energy is untainted, and, like that mountain stream, her presence washes over the devotee, cleansing the heart of old resentments and purifying the mind of toxic thoughts.

She is also **Sadyorāga Vivardhini**, the one who possesses the power of "instant" healing. Imagine a touch so potent that it can evaporate sorrow in a heartbeat. She is the force that promotes rapid growth and development. When we are stuck in a cycle of pain or stagnation, she acts as a divine catalyst, pushing us forward with a nurturing force that ensures our progress is not just steady, but swift.

The Divine Architect and Sustainer: Viṣṇurupā, Jaganmohā and Brahmarupa

In a magnificent display of her universal nature, the Mother reveals herself as **Viṣṇurupā, Jaganmohā** and **Brahmarupa**. She bears the form of Lord Vishnu, the Preserver, and Lord Brahma, the Creator. This signifies that the power to "still" an enemy (Baglamukhi's core power) is actually the same power that "sustains" the universe.

As **Jaganmohā**, she possesses the divine charm of Vishnu, a radiant presence that captivates the entire world. It is not a charm that deceives, but a beauty that draws the soul toward the Truth. As **Brahmarupa**, she holds the blueprints of creation. This tells the devotee that through her grace, we gain the power to reshape our own reality. She is the cosmic architect guiding us to craft a life of meaning and the sacred guardian who ensures our soul's work endures forever.

The Beloved of the Infinite: Haripriyā

Finally, she is **Haripriyā,** the one who is infinitely dear to Hari (Vishnu). This title highlights the inseparable connection between her protective Stambhana energy and the sustaining love of the Divine. Their bond is a profound union, ensuring that her fierce power is never used for the sake of destruction, but always for the preservation of life and the well-being of all. She is the 'Beloved' because she embodies the active, dynamic power of the Divine's compassion. When we call upon her, we are calling upon the very heart of the Preserver.

The Synthesis of Life and Light

Therefore, Maa Baglamukhi is the radiant dawn of Sāvitrī, the cosmic rhythm of Tripada, and the untainted purity of Śuddhā. She is the swift healer, the captivating preserver, and the creative architect of our lives.

She embodies the fundamental energies of the entire cosmos, offering us a path that is illuminated by the sun, cleansed by the stream, and protected by the highest gods. By her grace, we are not just shielded from our enemies; we are invited into the grand dance of creation and preservation, where we are nourished, healed, and led toward our ultimate spiritual blossom.

VERSE 11

रुद्ररुपा रुद्रशक्तिश्चिन्मयी भक्तवत्सला ।
लोकमाता शिवा सन्ध्या शिवपूजनतत्परा ॥ ११ ॥

Rudrarupā Rudraśaktiścinmayī Bhaktavatsalā |
Lokamātā Śivā Sandhyā Śivapūjanatatparā ॥ 11 ॥

आप रुद्र का रूप हैं, आप ही रुद्र की चेतना और ज्ञान की शक्ति हैं, भक्तों को वात्सल्य देती हैं, समस्त लोक की माता हैं, संध्या काल की देवी हैं, जो भगवान शिव की पूजा के लिए सदैव तत्पर रहती हैं।

You are the form of Rudra, you are the power of Rudra's consciousness and knowledge, you give affection to the devotees, you are the mother of the entire world, you are the goddess of morning and evening, who is always ready to worship Lord Shiva..

The Force of Renewal: Rudrarupā and Rudraśakti

Imagine a powerful storm sweeping across a parched and stagnant land. This is not a storm of senseless destruction, but a necessary force of transformation. Maa Baglamukhi embodies **Rudrarupā**, taking the very form of Lord Rudra—the fierce, wild, yet ultimately benevolent aspect of Shiva.

She is the energy that dissolves our limitations and shatters the stagnant patterns of our lives. When we are stuck in habits that no longer serve us or blocked by obstacles that seem immovable, she rises as the Rudra-force to break those chains. She is also **Rudraśakti**, the dynamic consciousness and potent power of Rudra. Think of her as a divine force field, an intense radiation of energy that repels all negativity. She acts decisively, ensuring that righteousness is upheld not through passive hope, but through the irresistible momentum of her divine will.

The Radiance of Pure Mind: Cinmayī

Envision a light so pure and so bright that it does not just illuminate objects, but illuminates understanding itself. Maa Baglamukhi is **Cinmayī**, a being composed entirely of pure consciousness and divine knowledge. She is not merely "wise"; she is the very substance of Wisdom.

In this facet, she dispels the heavy, suffocating darkness of ignorance (Avidya) that keeps us small. Imagine a guru whose eyes hold the depth of the entire universe, imparting secrets that can only be heard by the heart—this is the essence of the Mother as Cinmayī. She guides her devotees toward enlightenment by refining their perception until they see the world as she does: a play of light and spirit.

The Tender Embrace: Bhaktavatsalā and Lokamātā Śivā

Despite this formidable, world-shaking power, her heart remains a vast ocean of maternal love. She is **Bhaktavatsalā**, the affectionate mother who cherishes her followers with a love that knows no bounds. This is the "Vatsalya" rasa—the instinctive, unconditional love of a mother cow for her calf.

Think of a moment when you felt most vulnerable and imagine being gathered into an embrace of absolute safety and care; this is how she holds her devotees. She extends this nurturing further as **Lokamātā Śivā**, the Mother of the entire world. Her compassion is not selective; it encompasses all of creation. She is the universal parent who nourishes and protects every living being within her vast, golden embrace, ensuring that no child of hers ever wanders beyond the reach of her grace.

The Goddess of the Threshold: Sandhyā

Ma Baglamukhi shares a profound connection with the sacred times of transition. She is the 'Sandhya'—the Goddess of the confluence of dawn, noon, and dusk. These pivotal junctures of the day—dawn, noon, and dusk—are profoundly powerful for spiritual practice, for it is then that the veil between the mundane world and the Divine becomes most subtle.

In her form as 'Sandhya', the Mother facilitates our inner transformation. She stands with us during the 'Sandhyakal' of our lives—those phases of transition and uncertainty—and carries us safely from one state of being to the next. She teaches us that beauty and power are at their zenith when we are in the midst of the process of becoming something new.

The Eternal Devotee: Śivapūjanatatparā

Finally, she reveals herself as **Śivapūjanatatparā**, the one who is eternally ready and devoted (Tatpara) to the worship of Lord Shiva. This is a profound mystery: the supreme power of the universe herself in a state of constant devotion.

This underscores the inseparable bond between Shakti and Shiva. It highlights her role as the devoted counterpart who draws her strength from the silent consciousness of the masculine, even as she provides him with the power to act. Her devotion is the fuel for the eternal cosmic dance. She shows us that even the highest power is rooted in the act of sacred service and love for the Divine.

The Synthesis of Power and Devotion

Therefore, Maa Baglamukhi is the transformative storm of **Rudrarupā**, the decisive shield of **Rudraśakti**, and the illuminating brilliance of **Cinmayī**. She is the tender, universal mother **Bhaktavatsalā and Lokamātā Śivā,** the guardian of the twilight **Sandhyā**, and the model of perfect devotion as **Śivapūjanatatparā**.

She embodies the perfect balance of fierce authority and melting tenderness. She guides us through the fires of transformation with the wisdom of a sage and the affection of a mother, remaining forever anchored in her eternal love for the Divine. By her grace, we find the courage to let go of the old and the wisdom to embrace the new, safe in the knowledge that we are held by the Mother of the World.

VERSE 12

धनाध्यक्षा धनेशी च धर्मदा घनदा धना ।
चण्डदर्पहरी देवी शुम्भासुरनिबर्हिणी ॥ १२ ॥

Dhanādhyakṣā Dhaneśī Ca Dharmadā Dhanadā Dhanā ।
Caṇḍadarpaharī Devī Śumbhāsuranibarhiṇī ॥ 12 ॥

आप धन की अध्यक्षा देवी हैं, धन की देवी लक्ष्मी हैं, धर्म और धन की दाता हैं, धन स्वयं आपका ही रूप है, आप ही चण्ड दर्प (घमंड) को हरने वाली देवी हैं, शुम्भासुर राक्षस का विनाश करने वाली देवी हैं।

You are the presiding deity of wealth, Lakshmi, the goddess of wealth, the giver of religion and wealth, wealth itself is your form, you are the goddess who defeats pride, you are the goddess who destroys the demon Shumbhasura..

The Guardian of Cosmic Abundance: Dhanādhyakṣā and Dhaneśī

Imagine a celestial treasury, but instead of cold iron bars and heavy locks, it is a realm of light where abundance flows as freely as air. Maa Baglamukhi presides over this realm as **Dhanādhyakṣā**, the supreme guardian and administrator of all forms of wealth. She is the divine treasurer who knows exactly what each of her children needs to thrive.

She is also **Dhaneśī**, the living embodiment of Lakshmi's radiance. Picture a golden river flowing perpetually from her heart; it carries the bounty of material stability, but also the gems of vibrant health, deep-seated joy, and unshakeable inner peace. In this form, she does not merely 'give' wealth; she is the source of prosperity itself. She reminds us that true abundance is a state of being in which our worldly needs and our spirit exist in perfect, golden alignment.

The Architect of Righteous Success: Dharmadā, Dhanada, and Dhanā

Envision a light that doesn't just show you where the treasure is buried, but shows you how to walk toward it with integrity. Maa Baglamukhi is **Dharmadā**, the bestower of Dharma—the sacred principles of righteous living. She pairs this with her role as **Dhanada**, the giver of material means.

This is a profound spiritual lesson: wealth without righteousness is a burden, and righteousness without means can be a struggle. Like a wise mother who prepares her daughter for the world, she provides both the moral compass and the resources for the journey. In fact, she is called **Dhanā**—Wealth itself— signifying that every ounce of abundance in the universe, from the gold in the mountains to the wisdom in a book, is a physical piece of her own divine grace. By aligning our path with her wisdom, we stop chasing transient luck and begin to magnetize sustained prosperity. It is the ultimate shift from being a mere 'seeker' of fortune to becoming a 'vessel' of the Divine, where our work in the world becomes an effortless extension of her light.

The Crusher of Arrogance: Caṇḍadarpaharī Devī

However, her benevolence is never a sign of weakness. She is **Caṇḍadarpahari Devī**, the goddess who specifically targets and crushes the darpa—the inflated pride and blinding arrogance—of the wicked. This title links her to the fierce narrative of vanquishing the demon Chanda.

Imagine a force so powerful yet so subtle that it can effortlessly deflate a bloated ego and silence the boasting of the malevolent. She protects the innocent not just by stopping the hands of the wicked, but by striking at the very root of their malice: their pride. She reminds us that the greatest enemy of the soul is the belief that we are greater than the Divine Law.

The Defender of the Cosmic Order: Śumbhāsuranibarhiṇī

Finally, she is **Śumbhāsuranibarhiṇī**, the mighty destroyer of the demon Shumbhasura. Shumbha was not just a common adversary; he represented the ultimate threat to the cosmic order, a force of darkness that believed it could usurp the throne of the Mother herself.

Her victory over him is a testament to her unwavering, absolute power. When the negative forces of the world grow so large that they threaten the very balance of existence, Baglamukhi rises with a finality that cannot be questioned. She is the safeguard, the ultimate shield who ensures that, no matter how loud the shadows may scream, the light will always have the final, silent word.

The Synthesis of Grace and Justice

Therefore, Maa Baglamukhi is the supreme guardian of our well-being, the radiant queen of prosperity, and the mentor who leads us toward righteous success. She is the very essence of abundance, yet she remains the fierce warrior who shatters pride and annihilates the most formidable threats to our peace, ultimately restoring our soul.

In her, we find the perfect protector: she fills our lives with the resources we need to grow, while standing resolutely against the forces that seek to diminish us. She is the Mother who ensures her children are both prosperous and humble, safe in the knowledge that their wealth is protected by her mace and their hearts are guided by her light.

VERSE 13

राजराजेश्वरी देवी महिषासुरमर्दिनी।
मधूकैटभहन्त्री च रक्तबीजविनाशिनी ॥ १३ ॥

Rājarājeśvarī Devī Mahiṣāsuramardinī |
Madhūkaiṭabhahantrī Ca Raktabījavināśinī ॥ 13 ॥

आप राजराजेश्वरी हैं, आपने ही महिषासुर का संहार किया है, आपने मधु और कैटभ राक्षसों का संहार किया है। आपने ही रक्तबीज राक्षस का विनाश किया है।

You are Rajarajeshwari, you have killed Mahishasura, you have killed the demons Madhu and Kaitabh. It is you who has destroyed the demon Raktabeej..

The Empress of Empresses: Rājarājeśvarī Devī

Imagine a grand, celestial royal court, more magnificent than any human mind can conceive. Kings, emperors, and even the gods themselves stand in silent, humble reverence, bowing to the supreme sovereign. Maa Baglamukhi is **Rājarājeśvarī**, the Queen of all Queens. Her authority is not merely political or physical; it is a divine command that resonates through the very atoms of the universe.

Like a majestic empress whose wisdom is as deep as her power is wide, she reigns over the cosmic order with a perfect blend of grace and iron-clad authority. To worship her as Rājarājeśvarī is to acknowledge that no matter how chaotic the world may seem, there is a supreme, benevolent intelligence sitting upon the throne, ensuring that the law of Dharma is eventually upheld.

The Vanquisher of Chaos: Mahiṣāsuramardinī

Envision a field of fierce battle where the forces of darkness have grown so bloated and arrogant that they believe themselves invincible. Maa Baglamukhi manifests as **Mahiṣāsuramardinī**, the slayer of the buffalo demon Mahishasura. This demon was the embodiment of stubbornness, ego, and brute force—a chaotic entity that threatened to drown the world in darkness.

Like a valiant warrior who does not flinch in the face of terror, she confronted this formidable foe. In her victory, she did more than just win a battle; she liberated the cosmos from tyranny. She restored the balance of the elements and the peace of the spirit. She reminds us that no matter how "thick" or "heavy" our problems (represented by the buffalo) may seem, her golden spear can pierce through them in an instant. This victory is not merely a chronicle of ancient triumph, but a sacred template for our own internal liberation. By surrendering our stubborn habits and rigid mental constructs to her golden light, we realize that even the most immovable obstacles in our lives are merely shadows waiting to be dissolved by her presence.

The Guardian of the Beginning: Madhūkaiṭabhahantrī

Imagine the very dawn of time, the primordial moments when the universe was still in its infancy. From the ears of a sleeping Lord Vishnu sprang two terrifying demons, Madhu and Kaitabha. These beings represented the primal inertia and passion that sought to destroy the creator Brahma before he could even begin his work. These dual forces were not merely external mythological figures, but mirrored the internal inertia and conflicting desires that threaten to paralyze our own potential long before we even dare to manifest our purpose.

Maa Baglamukhi intervened as **Madhūkaiṭabhahantrī**, the destroyer of these two. She recognized that without order at the beginning, there could be no peace at the end. With her divine might, she eliminated these primordial threats, acting as the ultimate guardian to creation. She ensured that the cosmic order was established on a foundation of light, proving that she has been our protector since the very first breath of the universe.

The Master Strategist: Raktabījavināśinī

Consider the terrifying challenge of the demon Raktabīja. He possessed a dark miracle: for every drop of his blood that touched the earth, numerous clones of himself would rise, making him a seemingly endless army of one. Conventional weapons were useless against him.

Maa Baglamukhi, in her fierce and brilliant compassion, manifested a unique strategy as **Raktabījavināśinī**. She empowered the divine mothers, the Matrikas, to intercept and consume every drop of his blood before it could ever reach the soil. This ingenious act of spiritual "Stambhana" (paralysis of the enemy's power) led to his absolute annihilation. She proves to her devotees that she is not just a force of power, but a goddess of supreme intelligence and strategy, capable of overcoming even the most "infectious" and seemingly insurmountable evils. Much like her victory, this reminds us that we can stop the 'cloning' of our own challenges—whether it is a cycle of negative self-talk, repetitive stressors, or unethical desires—by intercepting the 'drops' before they take root and multiply into a storm we can no longer control.

The Ultimate Triumph of the Light

Therefore, Maa Baglamukhi is the supreme **Rājarājeśvarī**, the valiant **Mahiṣāsuramardinī**, the primordial guardian **Madhūkaiṭabhahantrī**, and the ingenious strategist **Raktabījavināśinī**.

She encompasses the totality of the warrior spirit. She is the sovereign who commands, the hero who confronts, the protector who preserves the beginning, and the strategist who finds a way through the impossible. By her grace, the "demons" of our lives—whether they be ancient patterns, stubborn habits, or multiplying anxieties—are met with a power that is absolute and a wisdom that never fails. She is the mother who wins the wars we cannot win for ourselves.

VERSE 14

धूम्राक्षदैत्यहन्त्री च भण्डासुर विनाशिनी ।
रेणुपुत्री महामाया भ्रामरी भ्रमराम्बिका ॥ १४ ॥

Dhūmrākṣadaityahantrī Ca Bhaṇḍāsura Vināśinī ।
Reṇuputrī Mahāmāyā Bhrāmarī Bhramarāmbikā ॥ 14 ॥

आपने ही धूम्राक्ष नामक दैत्य का अंत किया है, और भण्डासुर का विनाश किया है। आप रेणु की पुत्री हैं, महामाया हैं। अपने ही भ्रामरी, भ्रमरांबिका का रूप लिया हैं (जिससे आपने अरुणासुर का नाश किया था।)

You are the one who has destroyed the demon named Dhumraksh and destroyed Bhandasura. You are the daughter of Renu, Mahamaya. You have taken the form of your own Bhramari, Bhramarambika (with which you destroyed Arunasura)..

The Piercing Light of Truth: Dhūmrākṣadaityahantrī

Imagine a battlefield not of steel, but of shadows—a place shrouded in thick, suffocating smoke where you cannot tell friend from foe. This is the domain of the demon Dhumraksha, the "Smoky-Eyed One," who uses the power of confusion to overwhelm the righteous. Maa Baglamukhi manifests here as **Dhūmrākṣadaityahantrī**, the slayer of this smoky illusionist.

Like a sudden, piercing ray of dawn that cuts through the morning fog, she shatters the deceptive veils he weaves. She reminds us that the greatest danger often lies in our own confusion. By her grace, the smoke of our doubts is cleared, and we are gifted with the "sharp sight" needed to see the Truth as it truly is. She does not just defeat the demon; she restores the clarity of the soul.

The Destroyer of False Creation: Bhaṇḍāsura Vināśinī

Envision the architect of illusions, Bhandasura, who did not just fight the gods but sought to imitate their creation with his own twisted, magical constructs. He represents the ultimate 'fake'—the ego that tries to build its own kingdom through manipulation and dark power. Maa Baglamukhi rises as Bhaṇḍāsura Vināśinī, the one who dismantles his magical illusions atom by atom.

She proves that no matter how elaborate the 'magic' of the world or the ego may be, it cannot stand against the raw, primordial power of the Mother. She is the Divine Reality that collapses the house of cards built by our arrogance. In vanquishing him, she liberates our internal universe from the tyranny of our own delusions.

The Spiritual Lineage and the Cosmic Play: Reṇuputrī and Mahāmāyā

The Mother is revered as **Reṇuputrī**, the daughter of Renu (Renuka). This connection is a beautiful testament to the lineage of powerful, devoted women and the continuity of spiritual strength. It reminds us that the Mother's power is also rooted in a tradition of fierce devotion and ancestral wisdom. Alongside this earthly connection, she is **Mahāmāyā**, the Great Illusion. She is the master architect of the Lila—the divine play of the universe. While this "Maya" can bind the ignorant, for the devotee, it becomes a beautiful dance. As Mahamaya, she orchestrates the rise and fall of worlds, showing us that everything is interconnected. She is the magician who holds the secret to the trick, teaching us that when we love the magician, the magic no longer frightens us.

The Divine Hum: Bhrāmarī and Bhramarāmbikā

Finally, recall the unique threat of the demon Arunasura: with the boon of not meeting his end in any war, nor by any arms or weapons, nor by any man or woman, by any biped or quadruped creature, or any combination of the two. Maa Baglamukhi manifested a form that bypassed every defense: **Bhrāmarī Bhramarāmbikā**, the Goddess of Bees.

Transforming her divine energy into a vast, humming swarm of countless golden bees, she attacked from every direction at once, liberating the world from his oppression. This form is a magnificent display of her ingenuity and adaptability. She teaches us that even if our problems are like a swarm—small, numerous, and everywhere—she can become a swarm of light to meet them. She is the "Beating Heart" of the hive, the collective power of nature that rises to sting the heart of evil.

The Guardian of Clarity and Adaptability

Therefore, Maa Baglamukhi is the dispeller of smoky deceptions, the dismantler of the ego's dark magic, the carrier of the mother-lineage, and the queen of the cosmic play. Most beautifully, she is the **Bhramarāmbikā**, the humming protector who uses the most unique and creative means to ensure our safety.

In her, we find the power to overcome any deception and the wisdom to navigate the grand illusion of life. She ensures that whether our enemies are hidden in smoke, built on lies, or protected by clever boons, they will eventually fall before her golden, humming light. She is the Mother who adapts her form to meet our every need, ensuring that Righteousness always finds a way to win.

75

VERSE 15

ज्वालामुखी भद्रकाली बगला शत्रुनाशिनी ।
इन्द्राणी इन्द्रपूज्या च गुहमाता गुणेश्वरी ॥ १५ ॥

Jvālāmukhī Bhadrakālī Bagalā Śatrunāśinī ।
Indrāṇī Indrapūjyā Ca Guhamātā Guṇeśvarī ॥ 15 ॥

आप ही ज्वालामुखी, भद्रकाली (विनाशकारी शक्तियाँ), और बगला हैं जो शत्रुओं का नाश करती हैं। आप ही इंद्राणी हैं जिनकी पूजा इंद्र करते हैं, आप ही गुहमाता हैं, सर्वोच्च गुणों वाली गुणेश्वरी हैं।

You are the Jwalamukhi, Bhadrakali (destructive powers), and Bagla Devi who destroys the enemies. You are the Indrani whom Indra worships, you are the Guhamata, Guneshwari with the highest qualities..

The Alchemical Fire: Jvālāmukhī and Bhadrakālī

Imagine a great volcano, its deep, molten core pulsing with a raw, ancient energy. This is **Jvālāmukhī,** the fire-mouthed goddess. Her power is not one of random destruction, but of absolute transformation. Think of a raging sacred fire that consumes the debris of our lives—the old traumas, the stagnant fears, and the heavy impurities—leaving behind only the tempered, glowing steel of our true spirit. She is the intense heat of spiritual practice (Tapas) that incinerates the ego to reveal the gold of the soul.

Within this flame also dwells **Bhadrakālī**, the fierce and auspicious Kali. She is the embodiment of righteous anger, a force that dismantles evil with a terrifying, holy resolve. Like a warrior who sees injustice and strikes it down without a second's hesitation, Bhadrakālī within the Mother acts as a vigilant protector. She ensures that negativity is not just moved aside, but utterly dismantled, protecting her devotees with a shield made of the very shadows she has conquered.

The Secret of Silence: Bagalā and Śatrunāśinī

And here, we acknowledge her in her most potent essence: **Bagalā**, the one who seizes and stills. She is the **Śatrunāśinī**, the destroyer of enemies. We must look at this with the eyes of a seeker; our greatest enemies are often the "vikalpas" (doubts) and the "ahankara" (ego) that speak lies to us.

Imagine a force that reaches out and gently but firmly seizes the tongue of opposition, rendering every harmful intention powerless and every malicious word silent. This is the essence of her "Stambhana" power. She does not need to shout; her silence is so heavy and so golden that it simply dissolves the ability of the enemy to exist. By cultivating this inner stillness, we stop reacting to the external noise and start responding from a place of divine authority. It is the ultimate realization that when we are in alignment with the Mother, the victory is already won in the silence; we no longer need to debate, only to speak the limited, powerful words of truth.

Mastery Over the Senses: Indrāṇī and Indrapūjyā

Envision the celestial halls of the gods, where Indra, the King of Heaven, bows in reverence. Maa Baglamukhi is **Indrāṇī** and **Indrapūjyā**—the one worshipped by the Lord of the Deities. Yet, for the seeker, Indra also mirrors the Indriyas: the five senses that often pull us in chaotic directions, like unbridled horses.

By embodying Indrapūjyā, she establishes her supreme authority over our internal sensory world. When we worship her in this form, we are inviting her grace to sanctify our sight, our speech, and our perceptions. We pray that our senses cease to lead us into the shadows of worldly attachment and, instead, bow in devotion to the Spirit, transforming from restless wanderers into instruments of divine victory.

The Mother of Victory: Guhamātā

She is **Guhamātā**, the mother of Guha (Lord Kartikeya), the god of war and the commander of the divine armies. This connection reveals a beautiful truth: the Mother's power is the source from which all victory is born.

As Guhamātā, she births within us the inner warrior of our own spiritual discipline, ensuring that we have the stamina and the strategic mind to overcome any adversity that dares to block our path.

The Source of All Virtue: Guṇeśvarī

Finally, she is **Guṇeśvarī**, the mistress of all qualities (Gunas). She is the embodiment of the highest and most divine attributes— wisdom, purity, compassion, and nobility. Every virtuous thought we have is a spark from her infinite fire.

Think of a being who is the very definition of "Good." As Guṇeśvarī, she does not just protect us; she refines us. She bestows upon her devotees the highest qualities of character, ensuring that we do not just survive our challenges, but that we emerge from them as beings of radiant virtue. She is the gardener of the soul, pulling the weeds of our lower nature and planting the seeds of divine excellence.

The Golden Synthesis of Fire and Virtue

Therefore, Maa Baglamukhi is the transformative fire of Jvālāmukhī, the righteous sword of Bhadrakālī, and the silencing power of Bagalā. She is the sovereign of our senses, the mother of our internal victories, and the queen of all virtues.

In her, the fierce heat of purification meets the tender grace of motherhood. She is the golden fire that burns away our chains, the silence that stills our enemies, and the virtue that lights our way home. By her grace, we are transformed into warriors of the spirit, safe in her protection and shining with her borrowed light.

VERSE 16

वज्रपाशधरा देवी जह्वामुद्ररधारिणी ।
भक्तानन्दकरी देवी बगला परमेश्वरी ।। १६ ।।

Vajrapāśadharā Devī Jhvāmudgaradhāriṇī ।
Bhaktānandakarī Devī Bagalā Parameśvarī ॥ 16 ॥

आपने वज्र और पाश (फंदा) धारण कर रखा है, जिह्वा से मुद्ग़र (हथौड़ा) धारण करने वाली है। आप भक्तों को आनंद प्रदान करती हैं, आप बगला माता हैं, परमेश्वरी देवी हैं।

You are holding Vajra and Pash (noose), you hold hold Mudgar (hammer) and pulling the tongue of the demon. You provide happiness to the devotees, you are Bagla Mata, the Supreme Goddess..

The Thunderbolt and the Divine Restraint: Vajrapāśadharā

Imagine a goddess standing amidst the swirling clouds of the cosmic battlefield, wielding the very power of the heavens. Maa Baglamukhi is **Vajrapāśadharā**, the one who holds both the Vajra (thunderbolt) and the Pasha (noose).

The Vajra is the weapon of the gods that can never be broken; it represents her power to strike down the "hardest" of our problems—those deep-seated karmas and stubborn obstacles—with the irresistible force of lightning. Yet, she balances this with the Pasha, the sacred noose used to bind and restrain. This is her unique grace: she does not always destroy; she "captures" our wandering senses and binds the harmful energies of our enemies, rendering them harmless. She is the divine warrior who knows exactly when to strike and when to simply hold the world in a state of holy restraint.

The Hammer and the Tongue: Jihvāmudgaradhāriṇī

Envision the most striking and awe-inspiring display of her specialized power. Maa Baglamukhi is **Jihvāmudgaradhāriṇī**, the goddess who wields the Mudgar (hammer) while seizing the tongue of the demon. In our spiritual journey, the "tongue" represents the source of all conflict—falsehood, slander, and the deceptive chatter of the ego. It is the untamed impulse that often speaks before our wisdom has a chance to catch up, creating ripples of chaos that we spend lifetimes trying to smooth over.

By grasping the tongue and raising her hammer, she symbolizes the absolute **Stambhana** (paralysis) of the lie. She strikes down the "sound" of negativity before it can manifest into action. This extraordinary imagery teaches us that the Mother governs the very vibration of the universe. She silences the roar of the world so that the "Anahata"—the unstruck sound of the soul—can finally be heard. She is the guardian of Truth, ensuring that only the divine word has the power to echo in the heart of the devotee. This is the ultimate alchemy: the transformation of chaotic, destructive vibrations into the crystalline clarity of divine awareness, allowing our true self to emerge from the silence.

The Bestower of Ecstasy: Bhaktānandakarī

Despite these formidable weapons and her fierce stance, her internal nature is one of melting tenderness. She is **Bhaktānandakarī**, the goddess who brings immense, overflowing joy to her followers.

Think of a child who, after being lost in a frightening crowd, is suddenly scooped up into the arms of a loving mother; the relief and happiness that follow are the essence of "Bhaktananda." Her grace is a balm that heals the wounds of the battle. She reminds us that the ultimate goal of her power is not the defeat of an enemy, but the happiness of her child. She clears the path of thorns, ensuring our journey unfolds not in the shadow of struggle, but in the radiant light of her enduring peace.

The Supreme Reality: Bagalā Parameśvarī

And finally, the text brings us to the ultimate recognition: she is **Bagalā Parameśvarī**. She is the Supreme Goddess, the ultimate reality that exists beyond all forms and names. While we see her as the Golden Mother, she is in truth the Para-Shakti—the primordial energy that gives life to the sun, the moon, and the stars.

To call her **Parameśvarī** is to acknowledge her paramount position in the divine hierarchy. She is the source of all power, the architect of all silence, and the ultimate protector of all souls. Imagine the very essence of the universe, distilled into the form of this golden goddess, radiating an authority that is absolute and a grace that is infinite. She is the beginning and the end of our search.

The Final Golden Seal

Therefore, Maa Baglamukhi is the wielder of the lightning and the noose, the unique warrior who hammers away the lies of the ego, and the mother who fills our lives with the nectar of divine bliss. She is the **Parameśvarī**, the High Queen who reigns over the stillness.

In this final verse of her qualities, we see her as the perfect synthesis of strength and love. She offers us a shield that cannot be pierced, a silence that cannot be broken, and a joy that cannot be diminished. By her grace, we transition from the noise of the world into the golden sanctuary of her heart, where every enemy is stilled and every soul is set free.

VERSE 17

अष्टोत्तरशतं नाम्नां बगलायास्तु यः पठेत् ।
रिपुबाधाविनिर्मुक्तः लक्ष्मीस्थैर्यमवाप्नुयात् ॥ १७ ॥

Aṣṭottaraśatam Nāmnāṃ Bagalāyāstu Yaḥ Paṭhet ।
Ripubādhāvinirmuktaḥ Lakṣmīsthairyamavāpnuyāt ॥ 17 ॥

अष्टोत्तरशतं नाम्नां शब्द का अर्थ है "108 नाम।" अष्टोत्तरशत शब्द 'अष्ट' (आठ) + 'उत्तर' (बाद में) +
'शत' (सौ) से बना है, जो मिलकर 108 बनता है। 'रिपु' का अर्थ है 'शत्रु' और 'बाधा' का अर्थ है
'बाधा'। 'विनिर्मुक्तः' का अर्थ है 'मुक्त हो जाना'। इसलिए, यह भाग बताता है कि जो साधक
बगलामुखी के 108 नामों का पाठ करता है, वह शत्रुओं की बाधाओं से मुक्त हो जाता है। 'लक्ष्मी' का
अर्थ है 'धन और समृद्धि', और 'स्थैर्य' का अर्थ है 'स्थायित्व'। 'अवाप्नुयात्' का अर्थ है 'प्राप्त करना'।
इस प्रकार, यह भाग बताता है कि साधक को स्थायी धन और समृद्धि प्राप्त होती है।

The seeker who recites 108 names of Baglamukhi becomes free from
the obstacles of enemies. The seeker attains permanent wealth and
prosperity..

The Vibrational Key: The Ashtottarshatam

Imagine a devotee sitting in the soft glow of a lamp, their heart a vessel of pure reverence. As they begin to recite the **Ashtottarshatam**—the 108 holy names of Maa Baglamukhi—the very air around them begins to change. Each name is not just a word; it is a potent vibration, a specialized key designed to unlock a specific vault of her divine power.

By the time the final name is uttered, these 108 keys have opened a grand doorway to her grace. This practice is a sacred attunement; the seeker is no longer vibrating at the frequency of fear or lack, but is now harmonized with the golden frequency of the Mother herself.

The Spiritual Armor: Ripubādhā-Vinirmuktaḥ

Think of a shimmering, impenetrable shield of golden light forming around the devotee, woven from the very essence of the Mother's power. The verse promises that the one who recites these names becomes **Ripubādhā-Vinirmuktaḥ**—utterly liberated from the obstacles and afflictions caused by adversaries.

In our world, "enemies" are not always people; they are the negative influences, the jealousies, the legal entanglements, and the internal doubts that seek to pull us down. This recitation acts as a spiritual shield. Just as darkness has no choice but to vanish when a lamp is lit, the harmful intentions and "Stambhana" (paralysis) directed toward the devotee by others are dissolved. The seeker walks through the world with a divine "cloak of invisibility" against malice, granting them the ultimate freedom: the freedom from fear.

The Foundation of Gold: Lakṣmīsthairyam

Furthermore, the Mother ensures that the life of her devotee is not just protected, but deeply nourished. The verse continues with the promise of **Lakṣmīsthairyamavāpnuyāt**—the attainment of stable wealth and prosperity.

In our modern lives, we are all too familiar with the financial 'roller coaster'—where prosperity seems to wane and flow like a fickle tide, leaving us in a state of perpetual anxiety. But the Mother, as the custodian of the cosmic treasury, offers a different blessing. Imagine not a frantic scramble for more, but a steady, unwavering stream of abundance flowing into your life, creating a lasting foundation of well-being.

This is not the restless greed of accumulation; it is Sthirta—the unshakeable stability of resources. It is that quiet peace of mind which arises when one knows their needs are met, their family is secure, and their path forward is unencumbered. She provides the material grounding necessary to afford the soul the freedom to pursue the Divine, without the constant, distracting noise of scarcity. When the foundation of our material reality is firmly set in her grace, we finally possess the stillness required to listen to the subtle whispers of the soul, transforming our daily existence into a sacred act of worship.

The Sacred Surrender

This practice is far more than the mechanical repetition of names; it is a deep, soul-level connection. By reciting these verses, the seeker is essentially saying, "Mother, I surrender my battles and my needs to You."

Each name addresses a different facet of human existence— from health and speech to victory and peace. By invoking all 108 aspects of Divine Mother, the seeker ensures that no corner of their life is left in shadow. It is an act of total immersion in her golden aura, a surrender that paradoxically leads to the greatest empowerment a human can know.

The Promise of a Golden Life

Therefore, the regular recitation of these names stands as a supreme spiritual practice. It establishes a sanctuary of radiant strength that remains steadfast through every challenge, and it invites an enduring prosperity that blossoms and grows ever more vibrant with time.

It guides the devotee toward a life where the "noise" of opposition is stilled and the "music" of abundance is constant. Through these names, Maa Baglamukhi offers us her hand, leading us out of the web of adversity and into a radiant existence filled with lasting security, profound peace, and the golden grace of the Infinite.

VERSE 18

भूतप्रेतपिशाचाश्च ग्रहपीडानिवारणम् ।
राजानो वशमायांति सर्वैश्वर्यं च विन्दति ॥ १८ ॥

Bhūtapretapiśācāśca Grahapīḍaānivāraṇam |
Rājāno Vaśamāyānti Sarvaiśvaryaṃ Ca Vindati ॥ 18 ॥

इस पाठ से भूत, प्रेत, पिशाच और ग्रहों की पीड़ा से रक्षा होती है, यानी नकारात्मक ऊर्जा और ग्रहों के दुष्प्रभावों से मुक्ति मिलती है। पाठ करने वाला राजाओं या उच्च अधिकारियों को अपने वश में कर लेता है और सभी प्रकार की ऐश्वर्य (समृद्धि) प्राप्त करता है।

This recitation provides protection from ghosts, spirits, vampires and planetary afflictions, that is, one gets freedom from negative energy and ill effects of planets. The reciter brings kings or high officials under his control and attains all kinds of opulence..

The Fortress Against the Unseen: Bhūta-Preta-Piśāca

Imagine a world far larger than what our eyes can perceive—a reality teeming with energies that can often feel heavy, discordant, or draining. The verse speaks of **Bhūta, Preta, and Piśāca**—the spirits and energies that feed on our fear, confusion, and hesitation. For us, these often manifest as the lingering shadows of past trauma, the stagnant energies of our environment, and the 'doom-scrolling' anxieties of the future that drain our vitality.

The devoted recitation of the Mother's names acts as an impenetrable fortress against these forces. Think of a radiant, golden shield emanating from your heart, vibrating with such intensity that no lower or darker energy can endure its presence. Her names act as a divine 'cleansing fire,' burning away the clutter of the subconscious and ensuring your mental sanctuary remains undisturbed. She proves, with absolute authority, that no spirit—no matter how disruptive—is stronger than the Source from which all life flows.

The Mastery Over the Stars: Graha-Pīḍā-Nivāraṇam

Envision the vast, cosmic dance of the planets. Sometimes, their alignment is said to bring **Graha-Pīḍā**—the afflictions and obstacles that stem from unfavorable planetary cycles. We often feel helpless against the "stars," as if our fate is written in a language we cannot change.

But the Mother is the mistress of the cosmic law. The verse promises the **Nivāraṇam** (removal) of these planetary sufferings. When the sacred vibrations of her names fill your space, they neutralize the malefic influences of the stars. It is as if the Mother steps between you and the cosmos, adjusting the celestial frequencies so that you may walk through even a difficult astrological period with grace and ease. She reminds us that the power of the Divine Mother is greater than the power of any planet. Ultimately, she transforms our birth chart (Kundali) from a binding contract into a mere backdrop, allowing the radiance of her grace to become the true author of our destiny.

The Aura of Authority: Rājāno Vaśamāyānti

Furthermore, her grace reaches into the halls of human power. **Rājāno Vaśamāyānti** suggests that kings, high officials, and those in authority become favorably disposed toward the seeker. This is not about the dark art of manipulative control; it is about the "Vashikaran" of righteousness.

Imagine a devotee who, through their connection with the Mother, begins to radiate an aura of such quiet confidence, integrity, and light that even the most powerful leaders naturally offer them respect and cooperation. Like a sun that naturally draws the flowers toward it, your presence becomes an invitation for goodwill and favorable outcomes in all professional and social dealings. The Mother grants you the "royal" dignity that commands attention without saying a word. Ultimately, this is the recognition that when we are anchored in the divine authority of the Mother, the world instinctively mirrors that reverence back to us, proving that true influence is not taken—it is reflected.

The Fullness of Life: Sarvaiśvaryaṃ Ca Vindati

The verse concludes with a magnificent, expansive promise: **Sarvaiśvaryaṃ Ca Vindati**—the attainment of all forms of opulence. This is the ultimate fruition of our devotion.

Most of us, when we hear the word 'prosperity,' immediately think of our bank balance. But the Mother has a much larger vision for us than just the digits on a screen. Aishwarya is a profound term that encompasses far more than wealth; it is the richness of a sharp, discerning intellect. It also includes the vitality of a healthy body, the treasure of harmonious relationships, and the deep, spiritual abundance of a soul at peace.

Picture your life unfolding in all its dimensions, not as a static image, but as a vibrant, breathing garden in constant bloom. You are no longer merely surviving; you are thriving, supported by a lasting foundation of prosperity that the Mother herself has fortified.

It is the life we are meant to lead: balanced, abundant, and deeply anchored in the Divine.

The Harmonious Field

Therefore, the devoted recitation of Maa Baglamukhi's names acts as a potent shield against the shadows of the unseen and the turbulent influence of the stars. It fosters an environment of dignity and success in the material realm, while magnetizing the totality of divine opulence into your life.

At its heart, this verse conveys a profound truth: absolute security. In the presence of her sacred vibrations, negative entities lose their grip, unfavorable planetary transits lose their sting—so you can finally stop blaming that 'retrograde' for all your problems—and the doors of opportunity swing open with ease. She leads her devotees toward a life in which they are guarded by her power and overflowing with her abundance, walking through the world not as victims of circumstance, but as sovereign beings of light.

VERSE 19

नानाविद्यां च लभते राज्यं प्राप्नोति निश्चितम् ।
भुक्तिमुक्तिमवाप्नोति साक्षात् शिवसमो भवेत् ॥ १९ ॥

Nānāvidyāṃ Ca Labhate Rājyaṃ Prāpnoti Niścitam ।
Bhuktimuktimavāpnoti Sākṣāt Śivasamo Bhavet ॥ 19 ॥

इससे विभिन्न प्रकार की विद्याएँ प्राप्त होती हैं और राज्य (शासन या महत्वपूर्ण पद) की प्राप्ति निश्चित होती है। पाठ करने वाला भौतिक सुखों का भोग और मोक्ष (आत्मिक मुक्ति) दोनों प्राप्त करता है, और भगवान शिव के समान बन जाता है।

Through this, various types of knowledge are obtained and attainment of kingdom (rule or important post) is certain. The reciter attains both the enjoyment of material pleasures and moksha (spiritual liberation), and becomes equal to Lord Shiva..

The Master of Wisdom: Nānāvidyāṃ Ca Labhate

Imagine a mind that has become like a perfectly polished diamond, capable of reflecting every color of the spectrum. The verse promises **Nānāvidyāṃ Ca Labhate**—the acquisition of diverse and vast forms of knowledge.

By the grace of the Mother, your intellect sharpens and your intuition deepens. You find yourself able to grasp complex worldly sciences and deep spiritual mysteries with equal ease. if she removes the friction from your learning process. Whether it is the mastery of arts, the understanding of technology, or the deep secrets of the Vedas, the Mother opens the floodgates of wisdom, ensuring that her devotee is never left in the dark of ignorance.

The Throne of Influence: Rājyaṃ Prāpnoti Niścitam

The powerful vibrations of her names then manifest in the physical world as **Rājyaṃ Prāpnoti Niścitam**—the "certain" attainment of a kingdom or a position of high authority. For us today, this "kingdom" is our sphere of influence, our career, and our status in society.

Think of the devotee rising naturally in their field, their leadership qualities blossoming like a golden flower. This is not a kingdom won through greed or force, but one granted by the Mother because she has made you worthy of it. You gain the capacity to guide, to lead, and to inspire others, holding positions of responsibility where your word carries the weight of her divine authority. She ensures your success is not a "maybe," but a "certainty."

The Full Circle: Bhukti and Mukti

Most spiritual paths tell you that you must choose: you can either have the world or you can have God. But the Mother, in her infinite compassion, rejects this duality. She grants

Bhuktimuktimavāpnoti—both the enjoyment of the world (Bhukti) and the liberation of the soul (Mukti).

Imagine living a life where you taste the richness, beauty, and comforts of the material world, yet you are not a slave to them. You enjoy the fruits of your labour while simultaneously progressing on your spiritual journey. You are in the world, but not of it. She provides the "daily bread" for the body and the "eternal nectar" for the spirit, ensuring a holistic fulfillment that leads you eventually to break free from the cycles of limitation.

The Ultimate Transformation: Sākṣāt Śivasamo Bhavet

Finally, we arrive at the most profound promise of the entire hymn. **Sākṣāt Śivasamo Bhavet**—the devotee becomes equal to Lord Shiva himself. This is the pinnacle of the Goddess's grace.

It does not mean you become a god to be worshipped, but that your consciousness expands until it is as vast and as still as Shiva's. Your ego dissolves in the golden light of the Mother, and you embody the divine qualities of absolute wisdom, perfect detachment, and unshakeable bliss. Like a drop of water that realizes it is the ocean, your being merges with the Universal Consciousness. You attain a state of peace and enlightenment so deep that you become a living embodiment of the Divine on earth.

The Golden Conclusion

Therefore, the devoted recitation of Maa Baglamukhi's 108 names is the ultimate key to a perfected life. It opens the doors to all knowledge, ensures your rightful place of authority in the world, and balances the joys of living with the freedom of the spirit.

Ultimately, it leads you to that sacred threshold where you and the Divine are no longer two, but one. Through these verses, the Mother takes her child by the hand and leads her from the noise of the world, through the throne room of success, and finally into the silent, eternal heart of Shiva.

PART 3

Practices, Connections, and Enduring Legacy

The formidable Goddess Baglamukhi, a deity embodying potent spiritual power, draws an unending stream of devotees each day. It's a common sight to witness prominent figures – high-ranking officials and influential politicians – making pilgrimages to Baglamukhi temples, a testament to the widespread belief in her ability to bestow authority, victory, and protection. The sheer number of individuals who seek her divine intervention daily paints a vivid picture of the profound impact and perceived efficacy of Baglamukhi Devi's blessings in their lives. Her temples resonate with the fervent prayers and unwavering faith of countless souls.

Worship and Practices

Just as devotees across the spiritual landscape offer their heartfelt worship to a multitude of gods and goddesses, so too does Baglamukhi Devi receive the sincere devotion of countless individuals. The beauty lies in the diversity of these expressions of faith, with each person finding a unique and personal way to connect with the Divine. Whether through elaborate rituals, simple prayers, or quiet contemplation, every path forged with genuine intention and devotion holds equal merit in the eyes of the Goddess. Indeed, even the simple act of reverently uttering her name, imbued with sincere faith, is believed to be sufficient to invoke the benevolent grace of Devi Baglamukhi.

Mantras (Mool Mantra and others) and guidelines for recitation

The very essence of Baglamukhi Devi's power lies in the potent seed syllables, or bīja mantras. The most fundamental of these are

'Hleem' and 'Hlreem'. The syllable 'Hlreem' is particularly significant, as it is a composite sound that embodies the power of Manipura Chakra (the seat of divine fire and personal power), integrates with Vishuddhi Chakra (the center of purity and speech control), and is often linked to the grounding energy of the Muladhara Chakra. This composite sound directly signifies her power over action (Stambhana) and speech (Vak Stambhana). These powerful syllables serve as fundamental keys for invoking her divine presence. While this is a powerful starting point, a wealth of other sacred mantras dedicated to the Goddess exists, often best learned directly from a qualified Guru within the Baglamukhi tradition. These experienced practitioners, deeply engaged in Baglamukhi Sadhana, can offer invaluable guidance and initiate sincere seekers into the deeper mysteries and specific applications of these mantras.

While this text offers a glimpse into the realm of Baglamukhi mantras, its primary focus rests upon the Baglamukhi Ashtottara Shatanam Stotram – a sacred compilation of 108 names of the Goddess. Significantly, these names hold such inherent power and accessibility that anyone, regardless of formal initiation, can chant them with reverence. In fact, even a single name from this sacred list, when repeated with heartfelt devotion – for instance, simply calling out **"Pitambara - Pitambara"** – is believed to bestow the same profound benefits as the dedicated recitation of more complex mantras. The sincerity of one's devotion transcends the need for formal initiation in accessing the grace inherent in the Goddess's names.

The following are some famous, widely known mantras of Baglamukhi Devi:

Mantras are sacred sounds or syllables that possess spiritual power. They are an essential tool in the worship of Baglamukhi. The most important mantra is the Mool Mantra:

Mool Mantra: ॐ ह्रीं बगलामुखी सर्वदुष्टानां वाचं मुखं पदं स्तम्भय जिह्वां कीलय बुद्धिं विनाशय ह्रीं ॐ स्वाहा (Om Hleem Baglamukhi

Sarvadushtanam Vacham Mukham Padam Stambhaya Jihvaam Keelaya Buddhim Vinashaya Hleem Om Swahaa)

Let's break down the meaning of each part:

ॐ (Om): This is the primordial sound, the universal vibration from which all creation emanates. It represents the ultimate reality, the Brahman. It is a sacred syllable that invokes divine energy and sets a spiritual tone.

ह्लीं (Hleem): This is the beeja mantra (seed syllable) of Goddess Baglamukhi. It encapsulates her essential energy and power. It contains the essence of her ability to paralyze and control negative forces.

बगलामुखी (Baglamukhi): This is the name of the Goddess. "Bagla" means "crane" (symbolizing focus, stillness, and striking with precision), and "Mukhi" means "face" or "mouth." Thus, Baglamukhi is the goddess who has the power to seize or control the speech and actions of others.

सर्वदुष्टानां (Sarvadushtaanam): This is a Sanskrit term meaning "of all the wicked" or "of all the evil-minded." It refers to those who harbour negative intentions, cause harm, or act maliciously.

वाचं (Vaacham): This means "speech" or "voice."

मुखं (Mukham): This means "mouth" or "face," implying the power of expression and communication.

पदं (Padam): This means "feet" or "gait," implying movement, actions, and the ability to proceed.

स्तम्भय (Stambhaya): This is a verb meaning "paralyze," "immobilize," "stop," or "render powerless."

जिह्वां **(Jihvaam):** This means "tongue," specifically referring to the instrument of speech and potentially negative or harmful words.

कीलय **(Keelaya):** This verb means "seal", "nail," "fix," "bind," or "render silent." It emphasizes the complete silencing and control.

बुद्धिं **(Buddhim):** This means "intellect," "wisdom," or "understanding."

विनाशय **(Vinashaya):** This verb means "destroy," "annihilate," or "remove."

ह्रीं **(Hleem):** This is the Baglamukhi beeja mantra repeated for emphasis and to reinforce the Goddess's power.

ॐ **(Om):** The primordial sound, repeated to conclude the mantra with divine energy.

स्वाहा **(Swahaa):** This is an offering made to the divine fire during Vedic rituals. In mantras, it often signifies surrender, offering oneself, or invoking divine blessings and fulfillment of the mantra's purpose.

Therefore, a comprehensive meaning of the Moola Mantra of Maa Baglamukhi is:

"Om. Hleem. O Goddess Baglamukhi, paralyze the speech, mouth, and movement of all the wicked. Seal their tongues and annihilate their bad intellect. Hleem. Om. Swahaa."

In essence, this mantra is a powerful invocation to Goddess Baglamukhi, seeking her divine intervention to neutralize and render powerless those who harbor evil intentions, spread negativity through their speech, and engage in harmful actions. It also seeks to destroy their negative intellect and understanding. The repetition of the beeja mantra "Hleem" amplifies the Goddess's energy, and "Om" provides the divine framework. "Swaha" signifies the offering of this prayer and the desire for its fulfillment through divine grace. The Moola Mantra is considered the most fundamental and potent of all Baglamukhi mantras. It encapsulates the essence of her power and is the primary mantra used in her worship.

There is one more famous mantra of Devi Baglamukhi which is Sarv Karya Sidhi Mantra which is:

Sarv Karya Sidhi Mantra: ॐ ह्रीं ऐं क्लीं श्रीं बगलानने मम रिपून नाशय-नाशय ममैश्वर्याणि देहि-देहि शीघ्रं मनोवान्छितं कार्य साधय-साधय ह्रीं स्वाहा **(Om Hreem Aim Kleem Shreem Baglanane Mam Ripoon Naashye-Naashye Mamaishwaryaani Dehi-Dehi Sheeghram Manovanchhitam karya Saadhay-Saadhay Hreem Swahaa)**

Let's break down each part of the mantra:

ॐ (Om): The primordial sound, the universal vibration, invoking divine energy and auspiciousness.

ह्रीं (Hreem): This is another powerful beeja mantra (seed syllable) associated with various goddesses, including Baglamukhi. It embodies divine energy, illusion-destroying power, and spiritual awakening. It's often considered a heart-seed mantra.

ऐं (Aim): As mentioned before, this beeja mantra is associated with Saraswati, representing wisdom, knowledge, intelligence, and skillful action.

क्लीं (Kleem): This beeja mantra is linked to Krishna and Kali, signifying attraction, desire, fulfillment, and the power to manifest wishes and transform energy.

श्रीं (Shreem): The auspicious beeja mantra of Lakshmi, invoking wealth, prosperity, abundance, and overall well-being.

बगलानने (Baglanane): This is a vocative form of Baglamukhi, meaning "O Baglanane" or "O Goddess Baglamukhi" (with "Anana" meaning "face" or "mouth," emphasizing her specific form).

मम (Mama): Meaning "my" or "mine," indicating the personal nature of the prayer.

रिपून् (Ripoon): This is the plural accusative form of "ripu," meaning "enemies," "adversaries," or "obstacles."

नाशये-नाशये (Naashaye-Naashaye): This is a dual imperative form of the verb "nashayati," meaning "destroy," "annihilate," or "remove." The repetition emphasizes the intensity and urgency of the request for destruction.

ममैश्वर्याणि (Mamaishvaryani): This is a combination of "mama" (my) and "aishvaryani" (wealths, powers, prosperities, glories, or dominions). It signifies the desire for material and spiritual abundance and authority.

देहि-देहि (Dehi-Dehi): This is a dual imperative form of the verb "dadati," meaning "give," "bestow," or "grant." The repetition emphasizes the earnestness of the plea for these blessings.

शीघ्रं (Sheeghram): Meaning "quickly," "speedily," or "without delay."

मनोवञ्छितम् (Manovanchhitam): This compound word means "desired by the mind" or "wish of the heart."

कार्य (Karya): Meaning "work," "task," "deed," or "endeavor."

साधय-साधय (Sadhaya-Sadhaya): This dual imperative form of "sadhayati" means "accomplish," "fulfill," "achieve," or "perfect."

ह्रीं **(Hreem):** This powerful beeja mantra of Baglamukhi is repeated for emphasis and to reinforce the Goddess's energy and the intention of the mantra.

स्वाहा **(Swahaa):** An offering to the divine, signifying surrender and the invocation of the mantra's power to manifest the desired results.

Therefore, a comprehensive meaning of this Sarva Karya Siddhi Mantra of Maa Baglamukhi is:

"Om. Hreem. Aim. Kleem. Shreem. O Goddess Baglamukhi, destroy, destroy my enemies/obstacles. Give, give me wealths/powers. Quickly accomplish, accomplish my heart's desired work. Hreem. Swahaa."

This mantra is a powerful and direct appeal to Maa Baglamukhi for overcoming obstacles, neutralizing adversaries, and achieving both material prosperity and the fulfillment of one's deepest desires with speed and certainty. It combines several potent beeja mantras to amplify its efficacy in attaining all-around success.

Before chanting any mantra of Devi Baglamukhi, there is a practice in many traditions of chanting or Invoking on Meditating on Haridra Ganapati form of Ganesha to remove any obstacles in the path of meditation and Mahamritunjaya Bhairava for protection from all directions. The traditional practices may vary.

Guidelines for Chanting Baglamukhi Ashtottara Shatanam Stotram Stotram:

Time: Select a dedicated time for your practice, such as the serene hours of early morning or the tranquil evening. These periods are often favored for spiritual endeavors due to their peaceful and less demanding nature. While many find the span between 9 pm and 4 am particularly potent for Baglamukhi Sadhana, ultimately, you should choose a time that comfortably aligns with your personal schedule and rhythms.

Purity: Purity is not merely a rule of ritual; it is the prerequisite of reverence. To approach the Divine is to enter a state of heightened consciousness, and therefore, maintaining both physical and mental purity acts as a bridge between the mundane world and the sacred space we intend to create.

The Physical Bath: While taking a bath before recitation is not an ironclad mandate, it is highly recommended as a "ritualistic reset." In the Vedic tradition, water is not just a cleanser of the skin; it is a conductor of energy. A bath serves to wash away the Tamasic (inert/heavy) residues of the day—the exhaustion of the boardroom, the noise of social interactions, and the residual stress of our daily pursuits. It marks a clear transition: you are stepping out of the role of a consumer or a professional and stepping into the role of a seeker.

The Mental Cleanse: True purity, however, goes deeper than the physical. It is the practice of washing the mind. Before you begin your recitation, take a moment to intentionally "shed" the day's preoccupations. Treat your mind like a vessel that must be emptied of clutter before it can be filled with the nectar of the Mother's grace.

Ultimately, the act of purifying oneself is a signal sent to your own subconscious that "this time belongs to the Divine." Whether or not you are physically able to bathe, the intention of purity remains the master key. It is the sincerity of your heart—the desire to approach the Mother with a focused and clean mind—that she values above all else.

Posture: Sit in a comfortable and stable posture (asana), preferably facing east. A stable posture helps maintain focus and prevent distractions during recitation. Facing east is considered auspicious in Hindu tradition. the direction of the rising sun. Just as the sun heralds the birth of a new day and the dispelling of darkness, facing East symbolizes the awakening of consciousness and the movement toward illumination. By aligning yourself with the path of the sun, you energetically harmonize your internal state with the universal rhythm of awakening.

The Sanctum: Establishing the Sacred Threshold

The creation of a sacred space—a Sthapana or sanctum—is the final act of preparation. It is the boundary line between the profane (the mundane chaos of our daily lives) and the sacred (the timeless frequency of the Mother). By setting up an altar, you are not merely decorating a corner of a room; you are demarcating a threshold, a "thin place" where the veil between the individual seeker and the Universal Divine grows transparent.

The Focal Point (The Yantra or Image): Central to this space is the image or the Yantra of Maa Baglamukhi. A Yantra is far more than a decorative symbol; it is the geometric blueprint of the Mother's consciousness. Think of it as a resonant device—a mathematical condensation of her divine energy. By placing this at the heart of your altar, you establish a direct line of sight to the source. It serves as an anchor for the wandering mind, drawing your gaze and your focus toward the center, away from the peripheral distractions of the world.

The Energetic Laboratory: The environment you create around this focal point is critical. An altar is an energetic laboratory where the alchemy of Stambhan (stillness) is tested. A clean, quiet, and dedicated space tells your subconscious that you are entering a state of serious spiritual work. It is not about luxury or opulence; it is about intent. Even a simple space, if maintained with care, creates a resonance that supports the deeper states of meditation required to engage with the Mother's energy.

The Conducive Environment: When you step into this space, you should be able to instantly shed your roles—the professional, the parent, the social being—and stand solely as the seeker. By consistently using this same space for your recitation and contemplation, you charge the atmosphere. Over time, the space itself becomes a "battery" of sorts; the moment you sit before your altar, the vibration of the space will automatically assist in silencing your mind, making it significantly easier to bridge the gap between your limited awareness and the Mother's infinite grace.

Intention: Have a clear intention (sankalpa) in mind. Before beginning the recitation, take a moment to clarify what you hope to achieve through the practice. It could involve seeking safety, mastering one's circumstances, or achieving any particular wish.

The Sacred Alignment: Invoking the Guardians: Before one steps into the golden radiance of Maa Baglamukhi, one must ensure that the "house of the self" is in order. We often approach the Divine with a list of demands, while our internal garden remains choked with the weeds of past grudges and future anxieties. To engage with the powerful energies of the Mother, we must first establish a sacred ambiance through lineage-based attunement. This is not merely a ritual; it is a recalibration of consciousness.

Lord Ganesha: We begin by remembering Ganesha, the universal energy aspect that removes obstacles. Think of him as the Divine Gatekeeper—the aspect of universal energy that clears the psychic pathways of our mind, ensuring that the heavy density of material existence does not block our subtle perception of Truth. Without his grace, we are merely arguing with our own shadows.

Kuldevi and Kuldevta: We invoke the family deities to acknowledge the masculine and feminine energy aspects residing within our consciousness. These are the ancestral forces invoked by our forebears for the preservation and safety of the lineage. Honoring them is an acknowledgment of the "original code" of our soul. Importantly, even if one is unaware of the specific name of their Kuldevta or Kuldevi, the sincere intention of reverence remains paramount.

Matra-Pitra Dev (Parents and Ancestors): We offer deep gratitude to our lineage—our very DNA—acknowledging that we are the living continuation of our parents and ancestors. They are the roots; we are the fruits. Gratitude here is the fertilizer for our own spiritual growth. Furthermore, we offer humble prayers for forgiveness, seeking to heal the karmic debts of the past—both for the errors committed by our parents and ancestors and for our own transgressions.

Bhairav Ji: Finally, we invoke the protective energy of Bhairav Ji. If the mind is a messy room, Bhairav is the one who helps us sweep out the debris. As the aspect of universal energy that purges impurities, he acts as the ultimate guardian, rendering us "eligible"—a vessel clean enough to receive the intense, transformative grace of the Divine Feminine. In some traditions, there is also a tradition to invoke Hanuman Ji who is the embodiment of pure consciousness. And since a clean room is best enjoyed with plenty of light, many traditions also invite the presence of **Hanuman Ji**—the very embodiment of pure, unclouded consciousness.

With the internal terrain cleared by these protective forces, the seeker is no longer merely a reader; they are a prepared vessel, ready to stand before the golden radiance of the Mother.

The Language of Offering: Sacred Correspondences

Rituals are the poetry of the soul. The offerings made to Maa Baglamukhi—yellow flowers, turmeric, yellow cloth, incense, and lamps—are not mere material gifts; they are a sacred language. They represent an externalized conversation with the Divine, where the seeker communicates their inner state through these vibrant, solar-hued symbols.

The Alchemy of Yellow: As we have established, the color yellow is the frequency of the Mother's grace. Offering yellow flowers (Pītapuṣpā) and turmeric is a ritual of transmutation. The turmeric, with its antiseptic and purifying properties, mirrors the act of purifying the mind, while the yellow cloth signifies the "garment of wisdom" in which we clothe our intentions.

Incense and Lamps: These serve as profound metaphors for the seeker's internal process. The burning of incense represents the ego; like the incense stick, our arrogance and rigidities must be "consumed" by the fire of devotion so that a fragrance—a character refined by trial—can emerge. Similarly, the lamp (Deepa) is the light of awareness that remains after the darkness of confusion and the "enemies" of our own making have been stilled.

These offerings are the tangible markers of a deeper, intangible surrender. They are the artifacts of our devotion, signaling to the Mother that we are ready to leave behind the "heavy" habits of the past—our grudges, our cynicism, and our petty enmities—in exchange for her luminous clarity. We do not offer these items to "please" her in a transactional sense, as if the Divine could be bribed with flowers and cloth. Rather, we offer them to align our own consciousness with her frequency. By surrounding ourselves with these symbols of warmth, wisdom, and auspiciousness, we signal to our own subconscious that we are entering a space where the ego must dissolve, and the Divine must lead.

Pronunciation: Pronounce the names correctly. If possible, learn from a qualified teacher. Accurate pronunciation is considered essential. Incorrect pronunciation can alter the energy and meaning of the names.

Number of repetitions: The sacred Ashtottara Shatanam Stotram of Baglamukhi Devi offers a versatile framework for devotional chanting, inviting seekers to recite her 108 holy names with a frequency as personal as their devotion – from a single recitation to multiples like 3, 11, 21, 51, 108, or even more, fostering a profound and individual connection with the Divine.

Devotion: Recite the Ashtottara with devotion (bhakti) and concentration (ekagrata). Ashtottara recitation is not a mere mechanical exercise; it is a spiritual practice that requires heartfelt devotion and focused attention.

The Crescendo of Dhyana: The Meditation of Presence

Meditation or Dhyana is the bridge between the ritual act and the spiritual realization. Having cleared the space, purified the vessel, and established your anchor, you now arrive at the crescendo of your practice. This is where the "doing" of the ritual gives way to the "being" of the communion.

The Internalization of the Goddess: Meditation is the art of moving the Goddess from the altar before you into the sanctuary within you. It is not merely staring at an image; it is the act of internalizing her form, her golden radiance, and her sovereign stillness. When you focus on her, you are essentially practicing the Stambhan (stilling) of your own scattered awareness. By keeping the mind fixed on her, you are training the unruly horse of the intellect to stand still, allowing the higher consciousness to emerge.

The Spectrum of Chanting: Chanting her sacred names is the vehicle that drives this meditation. We engage in this in two ways:

Vocal Chanting (Vaikhari): Reciting the names aloud. This is powerful for the beginner or when the mind is turbulent. The sound vibration acts as a physical barrier against external distractions, saturating the atmosphere with the Mother's frequency.

Mental Chanting (Manasika): As the mind becomes quieter, you move the chant inward. This is where the true power of Baglamukhi manifests. Mental repetition allows the mantra to penetrate the deeper layers of your psyche, purifying the subconscious and clearing the mental debris that Bhairav Ji has already loosened.

The Experience of Grace: Meditation is not a passive waiting room; it is an active engagement. The goal is not just to chant, but to eventually listen to the silence that follows the chant. In those gaps, you experience her divine presence—not as a concept, but as a palpable, warming, and all-encompassing reality. This is the moment when the devotee and the Deity begin to dissolve into one another.

Ultimately, meditation transforms your puja from a repetitive ritual into a living conversation. It is in this stillness that you move from merely "worshipping" the Mother to "realizing" her within the very architecture of your own being.

Temples dedicated to Baglamukhi

While Baglamukhi is worshipped in many places, there are some prominent temples dedicated to her:

Baglamukhi Temple, Nalkheda, Madhya Pradesh: This is one of the most famous Baglamukhi temples in India. It is a major center of pilgrimage for devotees of the Goddess. It is considered a major Shakti Peetha.

Baglamukhi Temple, Kamakhya Temple Complex, Assam: The Kamakhya Temple, dedicated to Goddess Kamakhya, also has a temple dedicated to Baglamukhi. This highlights the importance of Baglamukhi within the broader context of Shaktism.

Baglamukhi Temple, Bankhandi, Himachal Pradesh: This is a significant and revered Baglamukhi temple in India. It is considered a major Siddh Peeth and attracts numerous devotees seeking her blessings, especially for overcoming obstacles and enemies.

Baglamukhi Temple, Ujjain, Madhya Pradesh: This temple holds unique and profound significance, situated within the **Prachin Siddh Shani Shaktipith** on the banks of the holy Shipra river. In the city of Mahakal, the energy of the Mother is uniquely intertwined with the energy of **Shani Dev** (Saturn). Devotees flock here specifically to seek relief from **Grahadosha** (planetary afflictions) and to resolve complex legal or court cases, believing the Mother here has a special capacity to "still" the malefic influences of the stars.

While these temples and other important locations are centers of devotion for Goddess Baglamukhi throughout India, the truest temple is the devotee's heart.

Connecting with Baglamukhi in daily life

Connecting with Baglamukhi is not limited to formal worship. Devotees can integrate her energy into their daily lives:

Ashtottara or Mantra recitation: Recite the Ashtottara Shatanam Stotram regularly or mantras if initiated or just her name - **Pitambara-Pitambara.** This can be done at any time and in any place, allowing the devotee to maintain a constant connection with the Goddess.

Meditation: Spend time in meditation, focusing on her qualities. This could involve visualizing her form, contemplating her attributes, or simply sitting in silence and attuning oneself to her energy.

Visualization: Visualize her form and her energy protecting you. This can be done throughout the day, especially in challenging situations, to invoke her protection and support.

Prayer: Offer daily prayers to Baglamukhi. This can be a simple act of devotion, expressing gratitude, seeking guidance, or asking for her blessings.

Righteous conduct: The most significant way to connect with Baglamukhi is to emulate her qualities – truthfulness, controlled speech, and righteous action – thereby integrating her divine principles into your life.

PART 4

Baglamukhi and the Science of Chakras

Introduction to the Chakra system and its role

The chakra system, a cornerstone of Eastern spiritual understanding, describes seven primary energy centers positioned along the spine. These vital hubs act as conduits for prana, the life force energy that sustains us. Starting at the base is the Muladhara (Root Chakra), anchoring us in stability and survival. Ascending, we find the Svadhisthana (Sacral Chakra) in the lower abdomen, governing creativity and emotions; the Manipura (Solar Plexus Chakra) in the upper abdomen, fueling personal power and self-esteem; and the Anahata (Heart Chakra) at the chest, the wellspring of love and compassion.

Continuing upwards are the Vishuddha (Throat Chakra), the voice of communication and truth; the Ajna (Third Eye Chakra) between the eyebrows, the seat of intuition and wisdom; and finally, the Sahasrara (Crown Chakra) at the head's summit, connecting us to spiritual consciousness. These energy centers are instrumental in regulating prana's flow throughout our being, significantly impacting our physical well-being, emotional equilibrium, and spiritual connection. A state of balance and alignment within these chakras fosters harmony and vitality, while blockages or imbalances can lead to various physical, mental, and spiritual disharmonies.

Baglamukhi's connection to specific chakras

Baglamukhi Devi, as one of the ten Mahavidyas, is deeply connected to the subtle energy centers within the human body known as chakras. Her energy and practices are primarily associated with the Muladhara Chakra (Root Chakra), the Manipura Chakra (Solar Plexus Chakra) and the Vishuddhi Chakra (Throat Chakra).

Here's a breakdown of her connection to these energy centers:

1. Muladhara Chakra (Root Chakra):

Location: Situated at the base of the spine.

Qualities: Represents grounding, security, stability, survival instincts, and connection to the physical world.

Baglamukhi's Influence: Directly, Baglamukhi's ability to provide protection and remove threats can contribute to a sense of security and stability, which are fundamental aspects of a balanced Muladhara Chakra. By overcoming obstacles and enemies, her worship fosters a sense of safety and groundedness in one's life.

2. Manipura Chakra (Solar Plexus Chakra):

Location: Situated at the navel region.

Qualities: Represents personal power, confidence, willpower, courage, assertiveness, and the ability to take action and overcome obstacles. It is associated with the fire element and the color yellow/gold, which are also significant to Baglamukhi Devi.

Baglamukhi's Influence: Baglamukhi is often depicted seated on a golden throne, symbolizing her dominion over power and authority, aligning with the energies of the Manipura Chakra. Her worship and name recitation are believed to activate and balance this chakra, enhancing one's inner strength to overcome challenges and adversaries.

3. Vishuddhi Chakra (Throat Chakra):

Location: Situated in the throat region.

Qualities: Governs communication, self-expression, truthfulness, and the power of speech. It is associated with the ether element and the color blue.

Baglamukhi's Influence: As the goddess who controls and stills speech, Baglamukhi has a strong connection to the Vishuddhi Chakra. Her power to silence enemies and turn speech into stillness relates directly to the energy dynamics of this chakra. Worshiping her is believed to purify the Vishuddha Chakra, granting clarity of communication, the courage to speak the truth, and the ability to express oneself effectively. The raising of Kundalini energy to the throat chakra during Baglamukhi Sadhana is also mentioned in some traditions.

Other Potential Connections

4. Ajna Chakra (Third Eye Chakra):

Location: Situated between the eyebrows.

Qualities: Governs intuition, wisdom, insight, psychic abilities, and the perception of subtle realities.

Baglamukhi's Influence: Baglamukhi's role in dispelling ignorance, illusion, and confusion aligns with the functions of the Ajna Chakra. By silencing negativity and revealing the truth, she helps to clear the mental clutter that obstructs intuitive knowing and clear vision. Some traditions associate her with the "third eye" opening, granting deeper understanding and the ability to see beyond superficial appearances. The focus on truth and the removal of obstacles to clarity in Baglamukhi Sadhana can indirectly stimulate and balance the Ajna Chakra.

5. Anahata Chakra (Heart Chakra):

Location: Situated in the center of the chest.

Qualities: Represents love, compassion, empathy, forgiveness, and connection. It is the center of emotional balance and healing.

Baglamukhi's Influence: While not a direct primary association, the courage and inner strength cultivated through Baglamukhi's worship can empower individuals to act from a place of truth and conviction, which are essential aspects of a healthy heart chakra. Overcoming fear and negativity, as facilitated by Baglamukhi's grace, can create more space for love, forgiveness, and compassion to flourish. Furthermore, the intention behind seeking Baglamukhi's help – often to protect oneself or others from harm – can be rooted in a desire for well-being and harmony, resonating with the energies of the Anahata Chakra. This divine energy serves not merely as external protection but also acts as a catalyst, melting our inner ego to reveal the purest form of love. Thus, the Mother's grace guides us toward a life where the vibrations of compassion and peace can be experienced in every single moment.

6. Swadhisthana Chakra (Sacral Chakra):

Location: Situated in the lower abdomen.

Qualities: Governs creativity, sensuality, emotions, and the ability to experience pleasure.

Baglamukhi's Influence: The connection here is less direct. However, the inner strength and confidence gained through Baglamukhi's blessings can empower one to express their creativity and embrace their emotions with greater authenticity, indirectly influencing the Swadhisthana Chakra.

7. Sahasrara Chakra (Crown Chakra):

Location: Situated at the crown of the head.

Qualities: Represents spiritual connection, enlightenment, and universal consciousness.

Baglamukhi's Influence: Ultimately, the goal of any spiritual practice is to connect with the Divine. By removing obstacles and granting inner strength and clarity, Baglamukhi's worship can pave the way for a deeper spiritual connection, indirectly supporting the opening and balancing of the Sahasrara Chakra.

It's important to remember that the chakra system is interconnected, and the influence of a particular deity can have ripple effects across multiple energy centers. While Baglamukhi's primary impact is often felt in the Muladhara, Manipura and Vishuddhi Chakras, her potent energy can positively influence the entire energetic body, fostering courage, clarity, protection, and ultimately, a stronger connection with the Divine.

A Note on the Architecture of Consciousness

It is crucial for the seeker to understand that the traditional mapping of chakras as lotus-centers within the spine is a pedagogical tool—a map designed primarily for concentration rather than a rigid anatomical blueprint. Diverse scriptures offer varying perspectives, revealing that these are, in essence, psychological and physiological landscapes of the human condition. The sequence of these centers may differ across traditions. The Lalita Sahasranama, for instance, invites us to a more somatic interpretation, mapping the subtle centers directly onto the tissues of the body: it identifies the Skin as Vishuddhi, the Blood as Anahata, the Flesh as the Manipura, the fat tissue as the Swadhisthana, and the bone tissue as the Mooladhara. This profound perspective urges us to look beyond the metaphorical; it suggests that the chakras are not distant, mystical points located somewhere in the ether, but are the living, breathing, biological reality of our own divinity. Here, consciousness does not merely 'reside' in the body—it expresses itself as the very chemistry and structure of our existence.

Baglamukhi for the Present Times: Navigating Contemporary Challenges

In today's intricate and often turbulent world, the age-old wisdom and potent energy of Baglamukhi Devi offer remarkably relevant guidance for navigating the multifaceted challenges we face. Her fundamental power to silence negativity, exert control, and reverse adverse situations provides practical applications across numerous aspects of modern existence. When it comes to managing conflicts, her energy can be invoked to quell discord and foster understanding, paving the way for peaceful resolutions by neutralizing aggressive tendencies and harmful communication. By embracing her grace, we do not just survive the storms of life; we learn to command them, transforming chaos into clarity with the precision of her divine silence.

For those grappling with seemingly insurmountable obstacles and persistent setbacks, establishing a connection with Baglamukhi can provide the crucial inner strength and unwavering determination required to persevere and ultimately triumph. Moreover, her unique ability to reverse negativity offers a potent tool for transforming unfavourable circumstances, dispelling negative thought patterns that hinder progress, and cultivating positive outcomes in various situations. Seeking her divine protection can also act as a shield against negative influences, harmful individuals, and the detrimental energies that can permeate the modern environment.

The efficacy of Baglamukhi's energy is particularly significant in our fast-paced and demanding world, presenting tangible solutions for overcoming hurdles, managing conflicts with greater clarity, and achieving success in our chosen endeavors. She bestows the vital strength and resolute will necessary to confront and conquer any obstacle that impedes our progress and aspirations. In situations of conflict, her influence aids in gaining a sense of control, fostering clarity of thought, and guiding individuals toward effective and just resolutions. Ultimately, by consciously aligning with her potent energy, individuals can unlock their inherent potential, gain the power to achieve their goals, and attain success in their respective pursuits.

Furthermore, a dedicated and sincere connection with Baglamukhi can catalyze profound personal transformation and genuine empowerment. She instills a deep-seated sense of self-confidence and bestows the inner fortitude and unwavering courage essential for facing life's inevitable trials and tribulations with resilience and grace. Her benevolent influence extends to our communication, aiding us in gaining mastery over our speech, enabling us to express ourselves with greater clarity and impactful intention, and fostering positive personal growth and holistic evolution.

Final message

Baglamukhi Devi, a unique and potent Mahavidya, wields the divine power of stambhana, effectively neutralizing negativity. As the revered goddess of dominion, she silences adversaries and reverses negative forces. Her worship is sought for protection, triumph over adversity, and the removal of obstacles. Connecting with Baglamukhi's transformative energy can foster significant positive change, bestowing self-assurance, inner fortitude, and the strength to overcome life's challenges.

Therefore, sincere devotion and receptivity to Baglamukhi's power can initiate profound positive transformation. By consciously engaging with her potent energy, individuals can unlock inherent resilience, realize their aspirations, and experience deep personal growth and fulfillment.

Embrace the formidable energy of Baglamukhi Devi with unwavering devotion and genuine sincerity. Establishing a deep connection with her divine essence unlocks a powerful source of strength, enabling you to transcend limitations, overcome life's obstacles, and cultivate profound positive transformation in every aspect of your life. May the abundant and protective blessings of Goddess Baglamukhi guide you toward victory, success, and a life of auspicious grace.

ABOUT THE AUTHOR

Deepika, the author, brings a robust background in Company Secretaryship (CS), Commerce (M.Com (BP & CG)), and Law (LL.B). Her deep interest in spirituality drives her writing, which she hopes offers empowering guidance without being preachy.

Beyond her professional life, Deepika finds joy in reading, writing, nature, and spending time with children. Her dedication to helping others is further reflected in her study of Mahavidyas and practice of alternative healing methods like Chakra Meditation, EFT, and Ho'oponopono. For inquiries, you can reach her at **contact@aroradeepika.com.**

GRATITUDE NOTE

To My Wonderful Readers,

My gratitude is immense for every one of you who opened the pages of my book. Your dedication and interest are a profound source of inspiration for me, and I'm truly honored that you welcomed my words into your experience.

The creation of a book is a shared odyssey, and it's sustained by the invaluable presence of readers like yourselves. Thank you for joining this journey and helping these narratives find their voice.

I invested my heart into every line, with the sincere hope that the ideas and insights within would spark something significant for you. Knowing that you had found practical guidance, a moment of inspiration, or even just a concept to reflect upon would bring me deep contentment. I encourage you to share your thoughts and reviews, or to connect with me via email at **contact@aroradeepika.com**.

Once more, my heartfelt thanks. Your support is invaluable, and I genuinely hope my words contributed positively to your life.

With deepest appreciation,

Deepika